2/B

SHREELA RAY

On the Life and Work
of an American Master

Shreela Ray: On the Life & Work of an American Master
Copyright (C) 2020 by Kazim Ali and Rohan Chhetri

All essays (C) authors unless otherwise noted.

ISBN: 978-1-7344356-1-0

Published by Unsung Masters Series in collaboration with *Gulf Coast, Copper Nickel, Pleiades, The Georgia Review,* and *The Asian American Literary Review.*

Department of English
University of Houston
Houston, TX 77204

Produced at the University of Houston Department of English

Distributed by Small Press Distribution (SPD) and to subscribers of *Pleiades: Literature in Context, Gulf Coast: A Journal of Literature and Fine Arts, The Georgia Review,* and *The Asian American Literary Review.*

Series, cover, and interior design by Martin Rock.
Cover photograph: Roger Alan Beck.

2 4 6 8 9 7 5 3 1
First Printing, 2021

The Unsung Masters Series brings the work of great, out-of-print, little-known writers to new readers. Each volume in the Series includes a large selection of the author's original writing, as well as essays on the writer, interviews with people who knew the writer, photographs, and ephemera. The curators of the Unsung Masters Series are always interested in suggestions for future volumes.

Invaluable financial support for this project
has been provided by the Nancy Luton Fund;
the University of California, San Diego;
and the University of Houston English Department.

UNIVERSITYof **HOUSTON**

SHREELA RAY

On the Life and Work
of an American Master

Edited by KAZIM ALI and ROHAN CHHETRI

OTHER BOOKS IN THE UNSUNG MASTERS SERIES

THE UNSUNG MASTERS SERIES

gULF COASt
A JOURNAL OF LITERATURE AND FINE ARTS

IN COLLABORATION WITH

THE GEORGIA REVIEW

COPPERNICKEL

A|L
A|R   The Asian American Literary Review

PLEIADES
PRESS

CONTENTS

INTRODUCTION

SELECTED POEMS

INTRODUCTION

A PREFATORY NOTE

We are elated that Shreela Ray, our mother, has been selected for this important and essential series of writers. We especially want to express our gratitude to Cornelius Eady and Kazim Ali for being her tenacious cheerleaders and further gratitude that now she is getting a wider reception. Eschewing university in the UK, she arrived in Missouri on a scholarship in 1960 when she was 18, in the middle of the civil rights movement. Throughout her life she would entangle both the Indian and American worlds in her work, as a humanist who affirmed the possibility of cultural transformation, refusing to cede the last, or the first, words to the West.

Contrarian but charitable, passionate and contemplative, she believed the poet's work distilled an entire life and world, like a miniature painting, in words. To Shreela Ray, the dinner party, the literary or political argument, the reading of theology and history, craft-making, marching for justice, all were a part of living as a poet in the world.

Her politics anticipated bell hooks and Gayatri Spivak, but she also resonated with British Utopians, writers like Christopher Lasch and Wendell Berry, and Edward Said. She was grateful for the Loreto Sisters in India who instilled a love of the mind and intellectual confidence. While a critic of religious hypocrisy and triumphalism, she was also a Christian who could read the Quran, and would often light incense along the statue of Ganesh, which she positioned near her typewriter.

She believed writing was a discipline, where meter and form help shape the craft, but she also would have cheered the different directions poetry has taken and the many new voices who have brought other worlds into words.

Thank you, reader, and may you find these documents and poems rewarding.

—Gawain de Leeuw and Kabir de Leeuw

SHEELA RAY: AN INTRODUCTION

Kazim Ali

Shreela Ray was born in Orissa province (now called Odisha) in India in 1942. Born into a mixed Hindu and Christian Indian family, she spent her early childhood in England and India and then moved to the United States for college in 1960, attending Bread Loaf while still an undergraduate student and then going on to the Iowa Writers Workshop to receive an MFA in Creative Writing. She developed relationships with many of the leading luminaries of the time who recognized her talent, among them W.H. Auden, Robert Frost, John Berryman, William Meredith, Isabella Gardner, Galway Kinnell, as well as Leslie Fielder and John Logan, with whom she studied at the University of Buffalo; Logan later wrote the introduction to the one and only volume of poems she published during her lifetime, *Night Conversations With None Other* (Dust Books, 1977).

Ray's work—written in pared down language, somewhat stark, sometimes tart, always sharp—was noted for its urbane and cosmopolitan phrasing, dark wit and the multiple lineages from which it drew. Her lineages include such Indian Anglophone poets as Kamala Das and Eunice De Souza but also the global Anglophone approach to the lyric of Seamus Heaney, Derek Walcott, or Fleur Adcock. At the same time Ray's poetry felt fully "American," combining a conversational, funny, loving tone with brash bravado, a committed "present tense"-ness reminiscent in many ways of second generation New York School, and deep philosophical inquiry especially in the later lyrics. The plainspoken becomes radical. For Ray to speak directly and plainly of emotions that would have been considered "unfeminine,"—emotions like ambition, displeasure, anger, or dissatisfaction—would place her within a context of women writers of the seventies and eighties that were breaking paths in terms of content and form.

Her poems were among the first poems I encountered in English when I was a young high school student studying poetry in western New York, first in the form of strongly smelling, nearly damp purple-lettered mimeographed copies of individual poems in a workshop at the public library taught by a local poet named Elaine Chamberlain, and then later in my high school creative writing class, courtesy of my teacher Mary Richert. It wasn't until decades later that I came to know that Mary Richert knew Shreela Ray quite well, and that during the summer after that first early creative writing class, Richert and Ray had gone on an epic cross-country road trip together in India.

During her graduate study in Buffalo, Ray met fellow student Hendrik De Leeuw, whom she eventually married; the two settled in nearby by Rochester, where she became part of a burgeoning poetry scene then centered around Al Poulin, a professor at Brockport State College who would go on to found the influential small press BOA Editions and the Brockport Writers Forum. She began publishing her work in national venues, including *Poetry*, in the mid 1960s. Her son Gawain De Leeuw remembers her as iconoclastic, idiosyncratic, and passionate. Mary Richert describes an energetic and highly opinionated Ray who chainsmoked *bidis*— handrolled unfiltered Indian cigarettes—and could argue equally passionately about politics, literature, philosophy, and culture—often into the late hours of the night.

I am struck by the fact that Ray's poem, "A Miniature for Hemant Kumar" may in fact be the first appearance of the Indian landscape in an American poem; and if it isn't the *very* first, then it is certainly the first by a writer of South Asian descent herself. It opens with that most familiar scene to an immigrant from a tropical country—that first shocked trauma of a full blown northern winter:

> The March snow is with us
> between the two stalled maples.
> Its rude white silence glitters.

> I will not come to terms.

The Indian landscape, which waits until the closing motions of the poem to make its brief appearance—in the form of both listening to the voice of an Indian singer and then remembering the warm Indian countryside— is somehow even more poignant for its contrast to the harsh and disruptive winter that the speaker finds herself inhabiting—like an alien—in the early part of the poem:

Your pure voice, Hemant Kumar,
that once could drug my peevish self
and make me move
once in the sunlight
once in the evening
like a dancer—
keens for an alien.

Hai Babu,
I should care
if the sun warms the fields and Radha's feet,
or that spring comes again to Kashi and Brindaban.

Indeed the poem's venue of a kitchen where food is being prepared, with the stove and oven warmth of its comforting and familiar foods and familiar music from the far-away home, might be the most welcoming room in the house for a subcontinental poet suddenly frozen in a Rochester winter, desparate for the Indian spring.

One is tempted to fall back on what may seem like anachronistic postcolonial buzzwords to describe Ray's critical milieu: liminality, hybridity, subalternity. But the truth of it was that Ray came from an already complicated background—mixed religious family (no small thing in India, as current events unfolding are brutally demonstrating) and also a mixed-culture/mixed-race/mixed-national marriage. Ray was keenly aware of the multiple realities she existed in simultaneously, always braiding together her landscapes and her contexts.

In the early "Poem to Gawain," certainly the anxiety around her still infant son's future romantic prospects evoke traditional Indian arranged marriages, some of which were fixed in early childhood or even infancy. In this case, the mother is making a space for the child, perhaps space she herself wasn't given by her own family. Another key gesture is the introduction of the philosophical into what is otherwise a private, domestic poem of a familial relationship. It's perhaps telling that Ray, iconoclast though she was, does not reference Freud or Sartre in thinking about the sundered self, but rather returns to the original, classical reference.

As Gawain De Leeuw points out, Ray was political in the extreme. She was strongly influenced by Third World Liberation movements of the sixties and seventies and was gravely disappointed, and further radicalized, by what she perceived as a global shift toward economic neoliberalism evidenced by Ronald Reagan's election, the first Gulf War promulgated by George H.W. Bush, and the early years of the center-right Clinton presidency. Ray's politics were anti-war, anti-imperial, and politically, socially and economically progressive.

As evidenced by her letters at the time, she was passionately devoted to the cause of Palestinian liberation, an opinion outside the political mainstream of her day. In a letter written during the Guf War, she wrote, ""Who voted the US world leader? why do we need one? Are we being attacked by another planet? And I am concerned for the Palestinians. I think it is over for them. My conscience will never rest." And in one late letter she even refers to herself as a "self-convert to Islam," but clarifies that it is mostly an ironic posture she feels necessary to adopt due to anti-Arab and anti-Muslim sentiment in the United States.

When I was preparing a lecture on Ray that I gave at the Library of Congress in the summer of 2019 as part of a series called "Secret Histories "(the response to which occasioned the realization that a volume such as this was needed), I contacted Mary Richert. She sent me an unpublished poem by Ray called "Fern" that she loved so much she memorized it. There was one phrase in the poem that Richert could not remember the exact words of and so had substituted a phrase she thought replicated the sense of the missing phrase, delineating it in brackets. This practice of receiving a poem by email that someone else has committed to memory—not having the actual text, I mean—demonstrated to me precisely the condition of the "secret history"—that texts were oral, committed to memory, repeated; that some texts, Sappho's for instance, were not preserved fully by history at all, and scraps is all we have left. In this case, I *remember* the poem—it's one of the ones that Elaine Chamberlain brought into that long ago workshop. It was one of the poems that seized my own imagination and that I myself had tried in the intervening years to find a copy of.

When I wrote to Ray's sons about the poem to see if there was a written copy I could include in the talk, her younger son, Kabir, wrote to say that he had several boxes of Ray's unpublished writings that his father Hendrik de Leeuw had kept in the years following Ray's passing. We found several manuscript variants for this poem, "Fern," in the folders, in its latest version published under the title "Anti-war," and have included it in this volume.

This is the poem the way Richert remembered it, a letter-perfect version of an earlier draft, with the portion she couldn't remember bracketed:

Light and sweet is the fern in the woods
and Gregory curled, sleeping by the fire

How was Khe Sanh possible?
How, Beirut?

Weren't there enough women with [souls on fire]
and tongues unflagging,

saying, "No, not this one.
And not this one, either."

This poem demonstrates well Ray's multiple lineages: she sets this very political poem, with its women-centered anti-war sentiment, in a deep woods setting, perhaps a camping trip. Gregory may be alone in the woods, or the nameless narrator may be with him, watching him while he is sleeping—a tender gesture of an intimate, whether friend, parent, or lover. It traffics in a common trope of political poetry—naming of a place or an event, without further elaboration. In original context, the poet may have been writing the poem with specific political intent and milieu, so much so that she could assume that an audience might automatically know the background and import of a place like Khe Sanh. Beirut, while perhaps more known as a place, at least historically, than Khe Sanh to the average American reader, also has more vagueness in intention: as opposed to the specific event of the Battle of Khe Sanh, the reference to Beirut is somewhat broader.

At any rate, the tactic of merely naming a place takes on different import in the information era: the references send one quickly to the oracle of the internet to seek background, context and clarification of these geographical and political references. Yet the poem does not hang there in the political sphere—it comes back to the very personal sphere of the one man in the woods. If the poem traffics a little bit in old-school gender politics (the man goes to war, the woman stays behind to protest) and a little bit of Lysistrada morality (a war will end if women can be strong enough to make it untenable), it is a product of its time.

Besides carefully preserving Shreela's manuscripts—both poetry and letters—Hendrik published a series of pamphlets featuring Shreela's work, beginning in late 1993 when Shreela's health worsened, and after her passing in 1994 and throughout the 1990s until his own passing in 2001. His sons remember him as much like Shreela: funny, compassionate, warm and charitable, and with deeply felt anti-racist political opinions. Frequent house guests spoke of the great hospitality of the de Leeuw/Ray household in Rochester. Hendrik, whom Ray met while studying at the University of Buffalo, had constructed a great garden for her—which Richert remembers Hendrik always referring to as "Shreela's garden," though he worked in the garden as much as she did. The house was always full of guests at evening-long dinner parties, in which Ray constantly served and circulated and kept conversations going, like an old-school salon hostess.

One of the guests at these salons was the poet Cornelius Eady, who as a young man, was a student of Ray's at Empire State College and for a time lived at the house. Eady has written that Ray "had a great impact on the way I look at what you should be doing with your students. You go for a sense of community—like-minded people sitting around being really passionate about the things they really care about." Later he wrote, referring to the organization supporting African American poets that he built with Toi Derricotte, that Ray's house "was one of the strands of the DNA that built Cave Canem."

Ray wrote at a moment when younger poets were mostly abandoning traditional prosody and traditional forms, though she herself occasionally introduced sonic patterns from her Anglo-Indian education. Consider these previously quoted lines from "A Miniature for Hemant Kumar":

Your pure voice, Hemant Kumar,
that once could drug my peevish self
and make me move
once in the sunlight
once in the evening
like a dancer—
keens for an alien.

The three heavy stresses of the first line in this excerpt slow down the line to the address, but are followed by the quickly moving iambic tetrameter of the following line, which is in turn slowed down by three more heavy stresses in the following line. The following four lines use dimeter to great effect. Ray was mostly writing free verse but she knew her music.

Of course silence governs Ray's body of work as well, not just the unsaid that makes her spare poems so powerful, but the silence that followed her one and only book. Ray had a family to raise and students to teach, true enough, and that is a condition that was shared by other women writers of the time, writers like Jean Valentine, Jane Cooper, Marie Ponsot, to name writers of a generation just earlier, or Carolyn Forche, Meena Alexander, and Marilyn Chin, to name a few others who were just younger than Ray and who also had periods of silence when they were not publishing. But there was also, of course, the silence that followed her death in 1994 at the young age of fifty-two.

There are easy answers of course: Ray was a woman, a woman of color, a poet writing in a complex context of a global literary heritage that may not have been easily understood by the American poetry readership at the time she published *Night Conversations with None Other* in 1977. Readers and critics didn't know whether to consider Ray an American poet or an Indian poet. The National Book Award jury was less confused. After requesting the manuscript for consideration (the award was by internal nomination at the time), upon learning that Ray was not a US citizen but had Resident Alien status, they informed her that she could not be considered. "My experiences and my language are of this country and its people—a nation of immigrants with whom I have spent seventeen years," Ray wrote to the Foundation in protest. Even with this setback, Ray's early career was storied. She was championed by such giants as Kinnell, Auden and Berryman. She had attended the single most premiere institution for creative writing at the time. Frost lunched with her at Bread Loaf. She was published in *Poetry* as early as 1966.

Despite, her admittance into these overwhelmingly white spaces, it was difficult for Ray, as a young woman of color, to be taken seriously. She recounts how the faculty, including Frost, would invite her to parties to which no other student was invited; later, she writes with an arch tone to her brother Miki of her time at Bread Loaf, "Mr. Berryman, a friend of mine who is married and a brilliant man who was in India and lectured at Cuttack, said I should stop being so intelligent and sit back and just let people enjoy looking at me but that would be awfully boring."

Shreela wasn't intimidated by Berryman or by anyone else. She continued to express her political views passionately, including in letters to the editor of the local paper, in the days before social media one of the main ways private citizens expressed their political views. We include one memorable exchange in the letters in which she argues with Noam Chomsky about the *fatwa* which had been placed on Salman Rushdie after the publication of his novel *The Satanic Verses*. Ray was of the unpopular opinion that the US intelligentsia was cloaking anti-Arab bias in the guise of their rallying cries for free speech. Chomsky conceded part of her point, but maintained the defense of free speech was paramount. They agreed to disagree, with Ray writing later, "Rushdie is a brilliant but flawed writer, ambitious and competitive in the intellectual *jet-set* culture and would probably like to be the youngest to win the Nobel Prize." She further speculated, "Some American publisher probably encouraged him at a fancy cocktail party, to put in the offending passages."

Her powerful commitment to progressive and radical politics, especially in international affairs, her erudition, scholarship, personal generosity, driving ambition, deep self-doubt, and incredible tenderness all shine through in the selection of letters presented here. Nostalgia for India, a frustration with professional setbacks, and a true horror for and anger at the military interventions of the Reagan and Bush years resonate throughout the later letters, in which she rails against the post-Gulf War "New World Order," though also becomes increasingly interested in comparative theologies, perhaps as a result of her elder son's pursuit of graduate studies in divinity. As her illness (sarcoidosis, which affected Ray's lungs) progressed, she grew more morose, disappointed in herself as a poet, and also as a mother. There is a plaintive letter to her old publisher Len Fulton, who had not contacted her in many years, desperately wanting to know why he no longer communicated with her. In response, he sent her a check for $41 overdue royalties; Ray returned the check uncashed. In a late letter to her son Gawain, upon his graduation from college, she wrote, "I wish now that people had not indulged me and told me I had talent. Obviously I don't, and certainly not enough to have warranted the time, effort and money (other people's) I wasted on it . . .. Now looking back, I see my life a gigantic hoax in which I am the main victim and perpetrator."

Still, even haunted in this way, Ray persisted, continuing to write poetry, and revise it carefully, long after she stopped publishing. She operated in a gift economy, opening her home to all, serving dinner, hosting literary salons which Eady remembers as being more important to him as a young writer than any publication or offer of employment. Indeed, the fact that Ray inspired the formation of Cave Canem is doubly inspiring: the organization Kundiman, dedicated to supporting the voices of Asian American poets often speaks of Cave Canem as one of *their* inspirations. So if, according to one of its founders, Shreela Ray was part of the DNA that built Cave Canem, then she is a foremother to Kundiman as well.

It was late in 2019 that I went up to White Plains, NY, where Gawain de Leeuw lives and went through the boxes and files of Shreela's letters and poems that Hendrik had so lovingly preserved. While *Night Conversations with None Other* was Shreela's only book, she had always intended to do another. She constructed a second manuscript that bore the title *Maggie Behaves Worse Than Expected*; the title is from a quote of George Elliot; there is no poem in the collection which refers to either a "Maggie" or to Elliot. Ray seems to have been dissatisfied with the collection and never seems to have sought publication for it. There were multiple versions of *Maggie* in the files, with varying tables of contents.

Shreela also (wanting to write something for her younger son since she had published a sequence of poems for Gawain in *Night Conversations*) wrote a twenty-two page long poem for Kabir called *Counting Cats* for which she actually had a publication offer, but various factors interrupted progress on the book and it was never published. In addition, soon after Shreela's death, Hendrik began publishing a number of small pamphlets of her work under the imprint De Leeuw Publications. In total he published thirty more of Ray's poems this way, in six pamphlets published between 1994 and 1998. Hendrik passed away in 2001.

Besides the poems that Shreela had envisioned as part of *Maggie Behaves Worse Than Expected*, the manuscript of *Counting Cats*, and Hendrik's pamphlets, there are around one hundred fifty more pages of unpublished poems in the folders. Shreela had continued to work on them throughout her life: the typed poems often existed in multiple versions, all with pencil- and pen-marked edits. In most cases, it felt obvious to us which was the final version: Shreela always pared down, polished a phrase, honed a poem like a knife on a whetstone. In other cases, we knew the final version by the font of typewriter Shreela used.

In the end, we knew that our goal was not to publish *everything*, but to present Shreela Ray in the strongest light possible, to present her as the master poet that she was. So what resulted was a selection of poems from *Night Conversations* and a selection of what we thought were the strongest and most representative poems from the balance of the work. Because of the length of *Counting Cats*, twenty-two pages, and its seamlessness which made it impossible to excerpt to advantage we elected not to include it. Apologies to Kabir!

In the end, we include here seventeen of the forty-seven poems that appeared in *Night Conversations with None Other*, seven of the thirty that appeared in Hendrik's chapbooks, sixteen of the poems Ray had intended to include in the manuscript she was calling *Maggie Behave Worse Than Expected*, and sixteen more unpublished poems from the balance of uncollected poetry. We didn't designate the uncollected poetry into sections, because Ray never finalized the manuscript of *Maggie*, nor did she arrange the chapbooks, besides the first one, "I sing because I love to sing," which was published while she was still alive.

The order of the unpublished poems is roughly chronological—not only were Hendrik's folders more or less organized by period, but Shreela typed all her poetry, and one can tell when a poem is from by how her typeface changes as she moves from an Olivetti, to a word-processor, to a printer. The single exception was Rohan's choice to move "I sing because I love to sing" to close out the poetry section; at any rate, it was the last poem Ray published in her lifetime, so it's appropriate it close out the selection here.

I want to thank, first and foremost, Mary Richert, who first brought Shreela's work to me and then kindly helped me prepare to work on Ray as well as facilitate introduction to Gawain and Kabir de Leeuw, Shreela's sons. Secondly, I have to thank Gawain and Kabir, as well as Kabir's wife Bianca, for their participation in this project, their care for Shreela's work, their hospitality during my trip to White Plains, as well as the time since then, patiently answering questions and helping us find photographs and other information. I want to also thank Lawrence-Minh Bui Davis of the Smithsonian who organizes the biennial Festival of Asian American Literature, and Jennifer Chang, who curated the "Forgotten Histories" lecture series which first got me really thinking about revisiting Shreela Ray. Kaitlin Rizzo took charge of the tricky chore of transcription, and while engaged in that work became so taken with Ray that she asked us if she could write an essay also. I'm so glad we agreed, as her beautiful essays joins other essays by Vandana Khanna, Tishani Doshi, Alicia Jo Rabins, and Rohan. Martin Rock designed the cover and interior of the book. Finally of course, I thank everyone at the Unsung Masters Series, most especially Rohan Chhetri, my co-editor on this project, whose care and devotion shine on every page.

I've always, from the beginning of this journey, thought of this book as a foray, a gesture, a sortie: there's much more of Shreela Ray's work to discover, and it's our hope that this book will function as a doorway opening out to a full-throated reevaluation and repositioning of Shreela Ray back into the landscape of American poetry, a master *un*sung no more.

SELECTED POEMS

from

Night Conversations with None Other

five virgins and the magnolia tree

When we were seventeen or sixteen
and sat in the tennis courts
under the Magnolia Campbellii
—one of the largest flowering trees in the world—
we had lost our senses and we talked our heads off.

Two were to be doctors!
Two students of literature!
One was about to die
and so could not make plans
to heal the world.

Except for her
I forgot the whole lot of you
and of what we spoke
in those hours between
Study Hall and Benediction.

And the good nuns—
if they only knew what
I remember
in the nights of this runaway exile—

the sweet, rich scent,
the cream and white of the magnolia blossom
eight inches across
and blooming strong
way above my head—

they would cut that tree down.

Night Conversations with None Other

for Louis Tsen

Too many wise damn fools tell me
you will come in time
frosty visitor.
Time is long and so is death
and there is left
the meantime to pass nobly.

The earth in my cries:
sleep-walking child
dropping his dreams
one by one.
Be gentle
gentlemen when
I shall have become too beautiful
ascending
seabird of the deepest
undivulged coffers of the sea
ascending
up
high
to nowhere
that is here
there, nor you

letter home

As the outward signs of winter leave us
the purple crocus springs up
in the neighbors yard and on the pavement
pieces of broken beds and picture
frames lie in a heap.

Your life is marked
with no lesser executions:
heat, rain, ice,
births and broken wrists,
deaths imagined and not imagined.

From time to time
let me hear from you.
"In June I shall sit for the examinations
There is talk of marriage in December."

But if word of me arrives during
the rain and the rivers turn gray,
I send my bitter angel to guide
you. Let your letter say,
"We have lost the records of your birth
and departure. Nobody
misses you in Bhubaneswar."

Poem (for my Father)

1

With my sari hiked above my knees
I trip over a stone near
the street. The blood trickles
from one knee in a thin stream.
Outside the gate the men carrying
their burden of death
stop and rest.

She is Durga, the terrible one,
Kali, the Black Mother,
her title—
the ferry across the ocean of existence.
Her long tongue is red with human blood.
She wears a girdle of human arms
and a necklace of human heads.
On either side of her, her
handmaidens grin as they tear
the limbs of children, and eat.

I go closer.
I have seen her beautiful
by another name;
dainty and small beside her husband.
Those about to die wear
a look of indifference almost
as they fold their hands in that gesture
of farewell, or greeting or supplication.

Goddess, Mother, Durga,
before the rivers deliver you to the ocean
already red with the blood of Asia,
I offer you one bleeding knee,
like straws my last two hands
to add to your ten. My wrists
have opened and closed four times
so I could see what the springs
of my body generate. In my
time I have also known galleries
of angels and demons.
Lady of harmonies, couple
my north and south.

2

The air is full with the noise
of crows and caterpillars dropping
from the moringa trees,
and the evening sky is red with dust,
dust of the city
dust of the river
dust of paper mills
dust of processions and
pollen dust and dust of
Tulsipur.

From a neighboring roof
a gramophone blasts out
the latest film hits
and from somewhere below me
a gentler voice sings,
perhaps by design—

What a stranger you are in your own land.
What a disgrace to forget your own language.[1]

I have deserved no less.
Because of the malice
my right foot bears my left
I stay and listen to the end of the song.

Why do you drift through unknown streets?
Whose house will you make your home in?

The weight of the night crushes
your chest. Radius and ulna separate.
The moon passes through your eyes.
Father I am shouting
can you hear me?
The dead do not know English.
They are the true Asians who lose
nothing but their lives and die
acre by acre.

You saw my fear go after itself
to learn the cause of all estrangements:
the first hunger and death.
What golden fawn, what book what
song could send me out like this,
cocky and dumb and so afraid?

You should have married me off at sixteen;
or if I was too ugly then
at twenty in the hope that time
would improve me: or if not then

---

[1]in original a seeming misprint "you own language"

at twenty-eight to an old Marwari who needed heirs.
I had hoped to read to you
but my words are impaled in the silence
and only the centipedes moving
among the brown rotting flowers
hear the scream and are heedless.

In the first flowering of grief,
I believed in rebirth.
The second time the loam dries
and the scales fall from my eyes
I swear
to serve the sick and hungry,
to toil the land,
to pray to Jesus
and if I marry
to marry of my own people
and never go to America
or if I do, to throw myself
like a burning page
into her rivers of oil.
Certainly I will forget
all this foolishness of poetry.

I remain where I am.
In the dark sleep of August
your bones take root and seek
my house and I in my half
sleep, with one ear[2] to the ground
hear the endless, soft hum.

---

[2] in original a seeming misprint "with one hear to the
ground"

3

Hearing of my arrival the squatters
wait burdened with melons and potatoes
at the edge of the forest.
I climb out of the jeep and go to them.
They see I am wearing trousers
and my hair is in a scarf.
They encircle me and salute me as your son.
The women wail and fall upon my neck
with their children, wide eyed and shy
clinging to their legs.
Shamed already by their gifts
I do not tell them
I am only a girl.

Outside the circle an old man
with a stick in his hands murmurs to himself,

The great man's son is always great
even when he is small
and the poor man's son is always small
even when he is great.

I see the circle tightens.
Beyond it is a jungle without roads
and soon it will be dark.
In the whites of a child's eyes
there are strong thin red ropes.

4

In the rice field a farmer points
to the elephant tracks and turd
scorched by the sun. A soft
warm wind moves through the fields.
There is a faint hum, a rustle
and my hair caresses my face.
I stand under the lookout from where
at night, the labourers armed with fireworks
watch for elephants.
But still they come
and crush the ripe grain
and raise their trunks to the sky
and glean the stars and feed
with the one hand which also
drinks and breathes and seeks.

A bullet would do the job, I think,
or is it true
as it is believed in the Cameroons[3]
that a man shares his soul with wild animals, a cow
elephant, his bush soul.
If it is true
they do not forget
they would trespass again:
move their great shadows through
the ready grain and repeat the motions
of elephants in flesh.
The ghosts of fathers and grandfathers watch.

---

[3] by "the Cameroons" we can only guess she is referring to
colonial unincorporated British territory called "the South-
ern Cameroons" which was eventually divided between
Cameroon and Nigeria

5

I do not know how I will die.
Maybe with a gift of flowers,
my head in a noose of jonquils.
Maybe as I step out of a car.
Maybe (it is often too possible)
by my own hand, shot, stabbed
for love or something hazardously
like it. Maybe even murdered.

My bush soul returns
carrying the cone and spearhead in my groin:
feeding in the cities and granaries
of this continent and shadowing
my hunter.

Who would want to hurt me?
This vast, black and kindly frame
that has stood on its hindlegs,
balanced balloons on its snout
and amused your children.
I have carried you and your burdens
and seen my body divided.
Here is a table from a foreleg,
a head gazes impassively from a wall,
the roses of my tusk grace a wrist, an ear.
But I do not come for revenge;
only to see the face of the hunter
and to reassemble myself.
If there is one here who knows me
give me the spear a second time
a third until I am
my own faintest memory.

A Miniature for Hemant Kumar

The March snow is with us
between the two stalled maples.
Its rude white silence glitters.

I will not come to terms.

I back up.
The glass behind me breaks:
ropes of red onions scatter on the floor,
but I never take my eyes off
and retreat.

Your pure voice, Hemant Kumar,
that once could drug my peevish self
and make me move
once in the sunlight
once in the evening
like a dancer—
keens for an alien.

Hai Babu,
I should care
if the sun warms the fields and Radha's feet,
or that spring comes again to Kashi and Brindaban.

Poem for Gawain

1

Half-breed
child
you are the colour of earth,
limbs of trees and deep rivers.
Only in them can you find sanctuary.

You remind me of my country,
its divisions, its inalterable destiny;
the white sands of Puri turning red,
the Deccan a tableland for scavengers.

I would like to save you,
to search for a second home.
There is none
because we are the poor
and the elders of the earth.
So use my body as a shield
and behind its metal sing
of the dark, so when death comes
you will think it is the sea.

And this casket, this body,
lie on it,
warm, familiar,
as though you were in your own room,
in your own bed.

2

If you should find yourself
one day
in love with a Chinese girl
in a café in Paris,
do not tell her
to stay with her own people,
even tenderly.

Follow her home,
stand under her window in the rain
but on no account give her
five dollars and send her off
in a taxi.
She may have more sense
and decide to go on living anyway.

And if you should meet Aristophanes first,
ask him,
when a man goes in search
of his sundered female half,
must she be of the same race?

3

I stand in the heartland.
From the south the ocean breaks in.
The desert blows toward the centre.

I do not know what to call it;
suicide, or murder or the natural
course of things,

when the wretched fall upon the wretched
for guns or for bread.

I will write this story for you
on a tortoise shell comb,
where the song becomes
something old and slow and hidden
in the carapace of your tiny
mortality.

4

What will you do?
You are the gold around my neck.
Star—

Learn American-English
live long
and be strong
and gun your mother down.

5

My father was buried alive
in the paddy fields
by his International Harvester tractor.
When they dug him out
his face was calm and he seemed
to be smiling.
How could I be sure
that mud hadn't transformed his mouth
and that the juice and grass of his land
hadn't masked his face?

For thirteen years I have carried
dead fathers, grandfathers, uncles
and the virgin halves of myself
in search of friendly ground.

Even the graveyards have no entry
for Marxist poets . . .

So I buried them all
in my head.

6

Mist in the morning
and mist over the hands below me
loading and reloading
mysterious shipments from the east.
Not the ancient commodities—
cloves and silk, but the heavy stuff
for the dinners and security
of the United States of America.

I start thinking about God.
At a time like this.
Above all things
in a place like this:
I think Bellona Christ is the greatest of gods.
He has even joined the Israelites.
All we ask of Buddha
is that he lie on his side
so we can carve lotus blossoms
on the soles of his feet.

I will speak of this always,
sometimes as we watch for the dawn
and the paper, and I see the red and blue
flag with its one white star
I cut with my own hands,
wrap itself around our makeshift staff.

I cannot tell you enough
that I am frightened.
My life is like the wastelands
Amerika leaves behind her.
And a people cannot be saved from this
by nails or sabbaths or chemistry
when every new infant is cradled
in the jawbone of an ass
bleached in that desert.

Night in April

The voice of the April wind addresses
the unmarriageable awake
in the real sleep of the body.
The windows are open
and the sleepy violets of the blood
stir towards the dark outside;
that final nakedness
in the silhouettes of doorways
and branches ascending and descending.
To stay would mean for always
I would remain to weigh and measure.

Let your breath enflame a second
marriage for that end. As for me
there is some other livelihood
when the essences of things call me 'sister'!

Before I draw back my wings and fall
into the keel of birdlike flowers
by god I will make a garden of this place.

Two Love Poems of a Concubine

1

Crawling into the black box on the wall
I call myself in the name
of fathers and friends and lovers
and most of all
in the name of one whose face
engraved on a stone turns
away from me and looks
into its heart.

2

Afterwards
when you turn your white back to me
I lie awake in the dark
remembering your words.

I wanted to keep some distance between us.

Had I no rights. Was something
wrong with me? I touch
my indian body lightly.
My answer comes
in the shape of a woman without breasts
who holds two smooth stones in her hands.

I am deformed and black
and greater than your sadness.

My anger is bound to my pride
with silk threads. I look
to the footboards and headboards
for saints to lift me up
to high safe places
for I know I know
if I lie in all the beds
of this world
I sleep with one man
who has his back to me.

towards a 32nd birthday

On Route 33 east
in the late afternoon,
after the rain, the fields
are half-lit by a strange sunlight
breaking through gray clouds.

Hobbema's "The Avenue Middelharnis.'

I grow afraid of my dreams—

you fleshed out in the thicket, suddenly,
returning to redress
eight years of my grievances;
my self-made
phalanx of bodyguards;
Tobias' angel turns away,
the fish stink,
the smooth gray stones
cold and hard
have lain under the peepul tree.
Theirs is a journey I may never make.

So I cry when they speak out,
in that natural secret voice
without judgment or accent
by all my names.

Foreigner

woman
mother

wife

jongleur.

The sun's waning shaft hangs above us all
like the sword of the other
archangel.
If it falls it would cut the road in half.

Saul: Four Poems

1

And Saul said unto him, Why
have ye conspired against me, thou
and the son of Jesse . . .?
1 Samuel, 22, v. 13

The room begins to take the shape of a vault.
A storm lashes the trees,
I try to keep my head as cool
as a vegetable garden in the summer heat
when the forked spirit longs to put
herself together and be still.

Last night I sat biting my nails
and cried like a girl in her time of the month.
Tonight I broke the clock in trying to set it right.

The darkness sits on the chair and purrs and yawns.
In the cat's infernal retina
someone is drowsing and I am no lioness to lay
my imperious length against the cub.

There is nothing of the cat about me:
the sleek body, the green eyes,
the cat habit of licking itself clean.
I only let him in as an old man forgetfully allows
angels or patience room in his house.

Thou knowest these things Lord
but I will speak.

If the gadfly does not know the whereabouts of the abyss,
the hand I beware, hold.

2

Epithalamion

The slightest brush of wings
sets the spirit humming,
swarming with stars.
When Orion unbuckles his belt
and rains the stars upon my head
there is no business wanting the dead.

The cyclamen of the year is under snow;
filament and another—ash.
Snow is ash,
woman and child,
ash is ash . . .
things I have touched.

How greedily they devour the blackness
and are devoured.
They never cry or grow absurd.
Your gold bangle brands the nape of my neck.

I am disturbed . . .
Is that blackness light?
have you forgotten you were snow-haired at birth?
I turn to salt and ash.

Armies of flies settle
upon the cut melon of our summer
to taste the red and sweet of our trouble
with satisfaction.

I have loved—it is true,
but it was nothing.
That you are gone is true
but it does not matter.

Besides, you would not like the taste of my mouth.
It tastes too much of nettles and indignation.

This is the hardest of all,
that we cannot choose to sacrifice
where the Law has decided.

3

My father when
the Moor stirs the constellations
of a foreign particular sky,
new rivers with his foot,
the eyes of the unkind father
are always upon him.

My father,
how many men in search of their father's asses are
made king?

Oh go to sleep and dream no more of daughters.

4

Some part of the sun will sure get us,
or perhaps, it will be the moon.
It doesn't matter which, so long
as the earth gets no perspective.

It buzzes and spins—
the little earth.

I break like a ship,
a ship of many voyages
and once much loved.

But on the glass bird in the hold
the bright sun breaks and breaks.

Remembering Michaelangelo's David

By these hands the vineyards ripen
and the beasts rise again in meadows,
to move off, desiring death again
in another time.

The women still observe him with impassive faces
and ungirdle themselves for the boy.
Old women in the delight of terror.
His eyes . . .

And dead young girls chafe against the cold,
wake to match the marble and breed
a race of beauty not for death.

How men regard him secretly in their
philistine awe, as he stands above
in anxious and terrible expectancy . . . is it . . .
of kingdoms and years of men.

He arrives always at the exact marble word
and the entire stone slays
the preposterous giant. When it roars
why should he care, this boy
who holds the covenant.

Absence and Others on Main Street

These . . .

from a well-stocked earth,
flies, footprints, crow's feet
the greater half of man and how many
creatures dead in the arms of time.

The only sun and I at noon
go mad, so tomorrow when the sun rises
this devious and cat blood
will be modified by its ninth death.

There are those who will always be after
pale centres of pistil, white stamen, yes,
in the ethical climate of these hemispheres.

But how far the wind carries
the dust of wild weeds:
capsules of poppy burst
and send here, there.

And what is the lord's plan
in the hip of the dark solitary rose?

And you know the way back.
Tarmac and planes overhead.
Flowers.

One belongs to convolvulus and one
compositae and one I
should know best, the inadequate
flowers.

The Scholiast
wrote of you Sappho as having been
very ugly, small and dark
but like the nightingale with deformed wings
enfolding a tiny body.

Sappho, a song before you drown
for the ferryman, a song
even for the girl who walks
in the scent of violets.

As for me—
there is always a boy
in the hyacinth
and because one summer in Vermont
I stood among the bulrushes
in the water
and suddenly the sun
pared me to the skin.

I felt the green world
like a HE
trip me with one blade

I gathered twelve rushes,
as if the twelve tribes of man
were in my arms,
singing in me.

Why is it wrong to ache for the sea?
Supposing the sun would say

"I am not bright enough,"
and sink fast?
You sleep in the eye of another summer,

whom time foraged and saved and proved
a friend. I speak and raise
the black rib of the phone
turning seashell in my hand,
and the shell in the ear awakes
and listens and moves at the sound
of the gentlest sea, far off.

I dread afterwards—
you would look on me
twisted and rotten
on a New England shore

and say
"Is this your sea?
The evergreen?
The way arms should hold?
Answer me.
Even the waters turn you back."

In sleep the indwelling sunflower is brightest.
The coquina is washed by the sea,

until he comes on gravel, his bruised
leg ascending the stair, his frayed
sleeve wiping his forehead.

Nothing is the same as before.

An Elegy

At last they uncoil, hold
bark, gum, a naked field
dandelion. The river does not stop
the fit. To falter,

to think it is not
the moment. Winds hurl down
an ounce of god, a loose rock,
a mountain weed, flower
of shattered stem.

They come after me, the birds, and spread
like elegies in a wood too dense
for undertaking, even alone.

Collector bees grow lazy.
Already the flies buzz. The earth cracks
where the worms toil

in one who dreamed of requital,
the sea or where rich sap
whelms stronger pines,
and the seed in the brain is permitted to bloom

without the jingle of metal rain, without
this green deep intrusion doomed
to earth's centre.

Louder and louder the greed
of water falling sucks at the nerve
holding me back like
the pickerel caught in weeds.

There is no escape from you unbearable
american benevolence. Let
Asia take her bastard child without complaint.

The waters of seven continents rush
towards me and over me.

2

The camps are silenced at night.
The terrorizing Midianites rest.
I go from light to light and come
to one desolate tent without incense

or flowers or hysterical women
and an old father cut down before his time,
and you in another country
thrashing the invincible net

that must imprison you.
I will always be there
bending backwards to see
my mortality reversed,

spitting upon itself . . .
what you would not touch.

Hands rise against the heavy moon
sinking fast to throat, breast,
thigh now foot tethered to the pole
south of earth and I hear
the wild hungry birds flutter
and the earth try pulling away.

From a Willow Cabin

It is early morning
and still no dawn. I try
to pass time thinking
of the brow of the Macedon,
the kiss that was Antony's
and full of death . . .

and you—where I am.

How disagreeable it is—this road
they have me take
                              guarded
by three storms.

There is witchcraft in the wind,
the verging meadows overgrown
with aconite and nightshade.
There is an insurrection in the rain.
Not a daisy has promised to be reborn.

Where is delirium or flight?
When they pin me to this black cross
how can I sing or dance?

If I were Nataraj, four arms wouldn't be enough.
My teeth would bite the rain,
these tired lids drink the sunlight I have dreamed.

I ask for fourteen berries of BellaDonna
to fly with the tongue of the meadowlark.

Trees

the un-netted growth
of saga
told tongue to tongue
past our chemistry
unfold once, twice, thrice
in me aimlessly reciting
"light, light"—

coherence.

The genius in the thicket is wild
seeking *the* berry in a bush
crammed with berries.

In the meantime, the Great Star
rises and sets on my back
like the angel of the miraculous pool
who stoops once, to one in a thousand years.

Teach me to be as patient as Methuselah
in eight-hundredth year before Christ.

God, they have barred the earth from me
and anger takes all night to close.

I look out of the window
at those distant possible roses
of twenty-two or twenty-three.

My would-be children cling to my skirts.
What will they do when they learn
I did not nurse them?

Like the moor, I was driven out for spain.

When you left, having nowhere to dive,
I let the fluid poison stain
the minotaur bed. The sword in your eyes
gives you away and I am not quick to move.

I have no guile or occult power
to seize the sun from its centre
and place it on your head or mine.

What do you care anyway for the crown of the sky
when my earth shudders in the light of your stride?

According to the roots of prophecy
the rotting tree was cut down.

The grounds will be perfect when
you walk with her.
The mid will not recall the sick
poisonous sapling of the tropics
only a botanist studies with interest.

The angel of history gave me
this little courage: remembrance
of the shudra Anarkali walled
to death for the love of Salim:
and Daniel delivered from the lion's mouth.

But tell me love, is my voice *so* soft?

At once the vision struck.

I could not wait to ride
the spindrift.
There was no one to stop
or rival me with arguments.

I reject the apocalyptic promise of him
excited at Patmos till his hair turned gray.[4]

I reject the indifferent metallic blur,
the brick with which this house is made.

I am nothing—
but averse to vegetable cells
and the impossible law which outlaws itself.

It was rain I leaned to hear
or someone shouting in the corridor, "shower!"
meaning the divine gold, the ocean spray?
I delayed at the window to make sure. There wasn't
a drop that even touched me gingerly, like you.

I stare at the trees;
strained to understand the language of the osprey,
migrations of domestic birds.

Tell me what is green and earth and rain,
what is mud and sky but do not tell me with words.

I only know a song when it comes
from the lips of old women, demented and crying aloud
to an insensible Polish god or whining,
"Kiss me nurse, before I sleep."

The night passes me on to disbelief,
and belief in the mercy of killing

---

[4] John the Divine, considered to be the author of the Book
of Revelations; thought by some to be the same John as
John the Evangelist.

them or me. We sing
in different keys.

All night I have watched
the orange flicker jammed
in my breast, smoke out,
be cancelled in the sea

Where dream fish receive
the gift of speech in my tongue
and the last anemone of the world
flowers in my ear.

My fingers turn to water.
A flower opening in its final hour
in the face of you—the Sun—

I am that other presence, a head
of semi-flowers, ray, disc. Burn,
burn for I am strange to the lover's kiss.

Bring me such flowers—
wild poppies.

Asia

Somewhere a boat no bigger than my fist
overturns
and drowns everyone in it.

I do not attempt to save it.
Would you?
Being what I am? Knowing what I know?

Each night, when the red moon and the darkness
marry
I stand on this far shore and mark
with an X the places
where the bodies are washed up.

And I shoulder them one by one—
safe conduct
to the vaults in my memory,
where they may lie in state
beyond contempt and further violations.

I build fires on the crosses.
The smoke stretches across these rooms
to make a ring around me.
I shall never know any other
enchantment
but this part mourning.

So I watch my speech and dress,
and do not look long at a man.

Hour of Darkness, Hour of Light

We have talked late into the night.

The fire is an old man
and the lamp on the street
has burnt out.

I beg you before I leave,
if you have more wine,
serve it now;
if you have more to say,
say it quickly and be cunning,
even a little immoral—
shine a knife in my eyes and ask,
"Do you mean it? How does it feel?"

Or
trouble my high bed with kings and tell me
that saints with spinning wheels
shall visit me.

Speak to me of fellowship and the love of God.
Anything. Anything.
Sustain my hand.
Light this page.

Address before an Empty Assembly[5]

Alif

It is enough . . . from the day I was born
in 1942 . . . it is enough.
My mother quickly voided her water
and when they weighed me I must have known,

(with the knowledge that has no mirror
and cannot see its own reflection;

with the knowledge that has no mouth
and therefore cannot sing or cry;

the knowledge without anvil or hammer)

I was born
victim and terrorist
in equal parts.

Be

Shumbu,

because you are the only image of God in this house,
and have endured the profanity of my Christian
teachers,

---

[5] The five sections of the poem are titled after the first five
letters of the Arabic alphabet, though Ray uses the Urdu
pronunciation.

tell me,
by whose scales does one measure suffering?

If my redemption can only come through suffering,
let me be damned.

If my redemption requires the death of one other
or six others,

I insist on being damned:
a cockroach, a grub.

But I will not forget to mourn. I will not forget.
But I will feel no more guilt.

Shumbu,

if my redemption cannot come from the work of my
hands,
the ordinary breath of my small asian life,
by loving a man, by bearing a son,
by the presence
of friends at my table,
(and why not?)
of even my enemies . . .

Give me the courage to use your knife
and furrow into the deep earth of my own body
and see with the eye of a grub, a God dancing like a
God
to the sound of my mere breath coming to a stop.

Te

After the first death . . .

I bring it all home.

Once there was a girl—

her soul popping out of her eyes.

She was so stupid that everytime
she gave herself to a man,
she'd say, "I trust you
because you are a poet or a liberal,
or if I'm very lucky, both."

Later she'd wipe off the spit
with a khadi washcloth—(pieces
of a grandmother's sari
from Independence days.)

and she'd chant, "Bapuji, I'm learning humility."

When she went into hiding,
I'd leave the back door open
and a bowl of rice and lentils
on the kitchen table at night.

She began talking funny:

"I sleep in the bosom of my father
who is older than Abraham."

Another time it was,

"Mohammed Darweesh,
I want to see your poems in the literary magazines
of the US;
your picture on the front page of the *APR*."[6]

She was sounding dangerous.
She couldn't find a job
and her poems returned with greater frequency.

Se

I showed her the PEN ad:

> *Members pledge themselves to oppose*
> *any form of suppression of freedom*
> *of expression in the country and*
> *community to which they belong.*

"That's the rub.
What country? What community?
Forsooth, what language?
Besides you've got to be
in a non-Western country.
I've thought of going to Russia,
of changing my religion,
of writing to Jerzy Kozinski

---

[6] Presumably Ray means Mahmoud Darwish, whose first
name in Arabic has only one letter of difference from the
name "Mohammed." In the earliest translations of Dar-
wish in English, which would have been the ones Ray en-
countered, his last name was transliterated as "Darweesh."
APR is the commonly used appellation of the prestigious
literary journal the *American Poetry Review*.

Dear Sir

You have not heard of me. One
of the harassment tactics of the KGB
is to make one unheard of. They
don't even put my name on programs.
That's harassment. But I am a very
important closet poet. In fact,
once I am in the West I shall be
instantly recognized as the matriarch
of the closet poets of the world.

Sincerely,
an endangered fellowpen,
Olga Volga"[7]

Poor girl, and over 5 years of shrinks too.
How can anyone believe her.

Jim

11 years now she's been dead.

No one gave her a bouquet of white lilacs.

I buried her in two pieces
as she'd asked:
her terrorist western head
is in the front yard
among the English daisies,
the gypsophila and delphinium.

---

[7] While Krosinzki was indeed the President of PEN America
in the 1970s, the poet Olga Volga is Ray's playful invention.

Her victim body is rendered to dust
in the back under the hibiscus
rose sinensis.

Twice a year
I turn over the earth
mixed with gypsum and manure.
The whole neighbor-
hood walks up and down in summer
to admire.

She sings at the top of her shrill
voice ragas for morning and evening.
No one listens anymore or understands
those eerie microtones, so she sings
for me, so I will not
forget my name and what I am
or from where I came, and go
inhuman
mad
not knowing.

Unpublished Poems

North Wind

How quickly it has become November.
Everything is happening too fast.
The evening comes too soon
and it's cold. Cold. Cold . . .. Last week
sunlight and strong winds
whirled and tossed the leaves;
and being so light already, I thought

if I wore an orange sari, the wind
would be a raja and carry me off
to the ruined citadel by the river
where once I had lived.
For a thousand evenings, perched
on the front steps of our house
I watched the college boys—
a comradely arm on the other's shoulders—
in rows of two or three or four—
go bicycling by ever so slowly . . ..

But what's the point of all this now?
To whom was I calling,
    "Wait for me,
wait for me'? To whom promising,
"I'll be back. You'll see"?
Was it the playboy? Was it the
zoologist? The dark one
    from Kerala?
They didn't even know,
I existed. They didn't even know,
I had flown to America. The world
has never been the same since.

2

Last week when my friends and I
called each other on the phone,
we talked about the weather, yes,
and our children too, books and things;
terrible happenings . . . some close
some far. From one I learned
of another in need of comfort . . .
of another in need of praise . . ..
And as we talked the wind
kept blowing and blowing,
swirling and whipping up
the leaves around the house
until it seemed the whole house
itself was spinning.

And each of us remembered Shelley
from way back in our separate lives . . .
and I'm sure, for a few seconds,
the spinning world fell silent
listening to itself prophesy folding
the leaves into its rich heart soil . . ..
A little Shelley goes a long way.

This week fewer leaves are on
the branches and the first snow
has fallen. There aren't many places
left for me to go; however,
next time my mind wanders
as it often does—it will go
in search of an ode, written
by anyone, to the North Wind.
If there are none, do not suppose
I have been chosen to write it.

Antiwar[8]

1

Calm and light honey was the spring
fern in the woods, and Gregory
curled sleeping before the fire.

How was Keh Sanh possible? How
Baghdad, Beirut? Were there no
free women to scream and shout, to make

common cause and strike if they must,
or else with a wall of aching arms
whisper without flagging once,

No. Not this one either.

2

In the morning paper there was a photograph
of three children inspecting
the fresh corpse of a youth
in El Salvador.

You and I have not killed anyone.
We have not served the hungry stones,
or poisoned children, burned their homes
or made them vanish.

So when we walk in Highland Park
redolent with lilacs, and up East Avenue where the

---

[8] See note to "Fern," p. 94.

copper beeches grow higher
than the minarets in Delhi,

say, how could we be wrong to kiss,
first, under the linden next,
the ginkgo next to the cottonwood?

Falling Asleep

The fan slices the night air.
My breath floats through the room
with pieces of letters, calendars,
pleas, unfinished poems.

Tomorrow remind me to remove
my name from the mailbox.
That this would end and despair
raise its last black flag.

If you remain, be a gardener,
naming nothing but after flowers—
larkspur, feverfew, columbine.
I do not think the dead are bitter.

It is past the time that I could be
provoked to tears by silence;
and those who do not know this
will learn to give up trying soon.

My heart is stone.
There is no place on earth I can
undo these years—fill them
with charity or a passionate marriage.

The closest sea is 300 miles away.
I wish I could go home, but now
changes frighten me and the language
is not one I write in anymore.

Those I loved most have died;
only a few names, a slight image
cuts though this space like a heavy
beam. That the dead aren't bitter
was a passing thought.

It is daybreak and only now
have I brought myself to this place.

Mother/daughter

When I look out and see the empty blue sky,
I want to anchor myself there,
so you would know me again as once
you did, when I was anchored
to your body's harbour.

What became of your dowry?
Your jewelry, your silks?
Who feeds you? Who holds you
under the turning fan in summer?
Under the turning starless ceiling?

I wonder if I shall see you again —
or at my death . . . would you come?
Go quickly and look at your sky.
And come; here, take back
what's left
                    of what you gave me.

Revolutionary

My father,
my last father in a distant earth,
you wouldn't recognize me today.
Who installed machine guns in my eyes?
Who turned my arms into weapons,
for everywhere I gaze is devastation.

If you send anyone with letters,
or love or money, warn them
beforehand, not to approach
me face to face. Let them say
my name in that special way,
and touch my hair with a sign
or flower of our country.

Journal

Among the things hidden
there was Vermont
and a boy
who said,
"I know it is raining
but let's throw our coats under us."

Later he confessed Pasternak
had said it first,
but it didn't matter.
Sometimes poetry just doesn't.

He could have been handsome
but for the sneer
at the end of that July.
And now my piecemeal life
is founded on poetry . . .
the beat of thundering hooves.

Ghalib

Ghalib sings,

the road is hard
for a lame man to walk,
and when there are
no stars in the sky,
he has only the emptiness
to go by.

So what
if he finds a mate
with a good pair of eyes.
On a black night such as this
they'd both land in a ditch.

Tonight,
for their sakes I pray
it's the same one,
or a meadow of green grass
or hay new mown.

Joppa[9]

I was there,
At Joppa, the sheet
that descended from the sky
Saint Peter saw crabs and crayfish
scuttling on the NE corner,
You did not know me then
You don't know me now.

Do not be afraid,
you who are you.

Allah is Allah is.

You are the wind

Allah is Allah is

There is no peace
and I cannot bear to be free
when all that I love is bound.

---

[9] Joppa (a latinization of its 4th century Greek name
Ἰόππη) appears in the Bible as the name of the city of
Jaffa. In the Greek myths it is the city where Andromeda
was chained to the rocks to appease the Kraken. Just south
of Tel Aviv, it was an Arab majority city incorporated into
the state of Israel in 1948, and eventually incorporated in
the municipality of Tel Aviv.

Kamala

Where are you going Kamala
little lotus, dark lotus,
so early in the morning?
Your slippered feet kick up
the dust but it's gold dust
that comes falling, a small
cloud at your feet
but don't tell me, don't tell me.

When you step out the wobbly
door of your house
into Khalasi Lane,
you can't make up your mind
which way to go to the post office,
because I know, I know
in my old bones, the fat
envelope in your hand must be
the letter to me, the one
that I have prayed for,
begged for, so let's go,
by the radio station
and Billimoria's General store
where we can stop on our way back
and see if a new Western
or Georgette Heyer have come in.
and I will buy you anything
that you want because look
you.

I have $50 American Express
my good husband gave me, but never

mind that. You can tell me
about the letter as we walk

at this very moment as I write this to you
even this I trip on a line,
a ribbon wound into my life so
what's beauty and what is truth I'm sure
I don't know anymore unless soon
very soon I will hold in my hand
a letter from you which will tell me . . . A car goes
by, a scooter,
a couple Romeos on bikes
whistle and leer.
No one in the world
can giggle or glower like you,
dark sister, little Kamala.
Let everyone beware.
Let no one stand in your way
for you are the voice
of your mother, the eye and hand
of your blind father and write to me
in their name, for they did not learn
to read & write for my letters
from America, to enter the 21st century

the wordless page I cannot burn
with my words, or turn into
an aery the grisly
right angle, the cordless scaffold
without a noose
tell me what blooms, what fruits
are in season

Fern

(3)

It will be spring soon.
I want to hold my son's hand
and walk with him in the cemetery
and the park, to look for the split-leaf pear
and the Persian Lilacs
for his first time.

Let him choose the tree
we will rest under
to dream a little,
to trust that the blue sky we see
through the tangled boughs
will bend to us in the evening—
a ripe orchard warm
with the world's fruits.

But to think 'warm' or 'blue'
is to remember how long
the cold winter was,
or how I looked in blue—
to think of loss, a world
without eternity.

And he, seeing me suddenly
inattentive, would grow estranged,
uncertain of his rival—
run off to trees we do not yet know,
or up the hill we have not yet climbed.
I would be loser twice in the same May,
to what was true, and what was not.

Fern[10]
(4)

Not that you change but learn
to bend like poplars,
not in the wind only
but as if
you heard music
or water running
A little to the north of you,
a little to the east—

That your roots spread out as far as the world goes.

Cuttack is a town
on the Bay of Bengal.
Meet me there,
wrap around some tiny,
sure thing—
stones of dolomite, cowries . . .

To be held by such roots
to be known by such violence.

---

[10] In earlier manuscripts, "Fern" was a poem in four parts.
Ray later took the first two sections and made them into a
different poem, "Antiwar." We offer the remaining sections
under the original title.

Zero at 32

The days of my life split
in half, and will not speak to each other.
I myself am speechless.

Each calls himself Zero,
and hurls obscenities at the other
in a language neither can understand.
The blind one believes
his eyes are at the back of his head.
The other leaves the country
and is thrown out of posh restaurants.

I often fall asleep in the snow dreaming
that someday
they will shake hands, like two good losers
and I shall be whole again.

Kafka 2

How often have you heard me say
my father,
enough's enough.
I won't play confidante of God
or Satan anymore; the tribe's outcaste and
the tribe's prize.

Sisters, elder brothers in the same midnight
have appeared occasionally
to warn me. One had calloused feet
and wore yellow moccasins. He held
a sheaf of my first poems in his hands.

            "Ours is a task
of infinite loneliness. It's bad
enough for a man, even worse for a woman.
Are you sure you want this?"

And long before he flew off a bridge
in St. Paul, Minnesota, another said:
"Go home go home before
this country destroys you."

Echo

Today was the worst day of my life
until I read the prison poems of a man
who died when I was twenty-one.

How much he loved this world
its blue mountains, its small
and great rivers.

How much he loved his country,
so many of its men,
its women
hunched in pain, or from a sleep
they would never awake.

And how much he loved his wife—
her courage, her letters, her red hair.

So, resolving to change my life,
I fell in love with a man
I have never met,
for painting blue flowers
on the back of a porcelain mule.

But the tall narcissus lies
where it had fallen trailing the sun.
It's white head lolls over the table's edge.

So simply and quietly was I spoken to
that I took up my human place
and have no thought as yet
of putting it aside.

*Nazim Hikmet
b. 1902-1963
sentenced for 35 years
(reduced to 25 yrs., four months)

Stations

But I am transformed into water—
swish about your feet, between your toes,
Look, I am at your Bernini calves,
I am at your knees when you recognize me,
and the tide keeps rising.
It's ok, ok. Don't worry so much.
I know where to stop.

But one can sleep only for so long
and there is the other side to the poem—
that is when I wake up and the world
is really a god awful place.
I'm alone at the trailways station in Buffalo,
crying, I love you I love you, I love you
and I don't even remember your name
and you don't know anything.

"Inside this endless winter dirt . . ."

Inside this endless winter dirt
beneath the snow, if snow,
not imaginings of New England,
I see the ends of summer, infant carriages
limbs of trees, bits of portulaca leaves burnt

For two years nothing but silence.
Every year when winter comes around
I catch it at its end

For two years I have known nothing but silence.
Inside this endless winter dirt
bits of summer things begin to appear,
with voices of their own sounding impotent.
They would start over again delivered by tongs.

There have been many false starts,
I can hardly count them all
letters and phone calls
as though your voice, your limbs
would reorder my life

*

There is no merciful way to put a country to sleep
but I hope in the death of the oppressor

To let the boats loose when the tide came in
and the islets about us drowned but where the heron
stood, I called Marcus Aurelius

night watch

There is no profit in waiting
for Orion to unbuckle his belt
and shed stars upon my head.
That is no business, wanting the dead.

But perhaps one remains to be surprised
that with all this time
something may happen to hold for a while
or at least until I grow obdurate.

No. This is the end
or very near it. It's been long
since I looked out the window
at nothing for the voice.

There were the poles black obelisks
and silver in moonlight
and that show-off Orion with his dog fido.
The lonely night-heron without mate

forgetful in the field beyond the gates
did not hear. Anyway
as Samuel answered as a boy
so did I, "speak speak."

The way we are

Somewhere in Arkansas on a Sunday morning
the good people prepare for Church.
I too get ready to pray for my father
who spent a quarter of his salary
on my education.

I had composed a special text for my mother.
She cried when she packed
her engagement dress in the black
trunk. May her closets fill
with kitchen gadgets from America.

She had such high hopes for me.
Come back and marry a king;
maybe Gandhi's only grandson!

Baptist USA here I come!
Enter Charlene:
"The family would prefer you don't come
to Church. Please understand the way
things are in small towns."

The children of Ham and of Ishmael
have always taken up the burden
of good manners to understand
that sermons are a bore and I'd fall
asleep on the coir mat

on my hands and knees between the opening
prayer and letter to the Galatians.
So I spent the morning on a swing.

The sky opened like the throat of God
containing all the truth the world
turns on, and I groped
descending in the universal ichor,
with both feet on the ground.

No Man's Land

From the season that outraged one death
I enter another and mud of its fields
cling to my boots. Wormy apples bounce
onto the road. I walk to where I must
and meet the wary disciple and scholar
who credit me with more villainies
than can be handled in a year.

Wherever we stand Krishna, I hear
the song of the boatmen returning
home with hay.

Every year the gods are drowned in the rivers.
Children lay their heads
in the concave chests of their mothers
and dream
infant, material dreams.

Once standing on a high mound
above babel, I watched a fair
and the festivals of boats at dusk.
A dog limped up the hill and fell.

My country sometimes I wish
for a last storm or flood or fire,
where the slaughterpen of the world
opens to another day and the vermilion
sun dies in the Arabian Sea.

For Margaret Burke-White

I have no fear of thieves.
My ghosts are safe whimpering
in their allotted corners.

I contemplate the anger of pigeons—
their ruffled feathers,
the necessity of cats.
Oh,
and the boards shine their hard nails.

My eyes close over fish
swimming and spawning until
the rose-coloured day.
I recognize the face of someone
I thought missing.

Vultures grown too heavy to fly,
sun themselves on the high parapets
of another city.

The Road to Puri[11]

Earth scented by the first rains,
sweetness of red clay,
wet leaves and the sea approaching.

I turn to clay and sleep.
                              Paddy fields
ripple in the blood,
bone and tissue succumb
to tamarind and shad.

I eat gram out of cones made
from examination papers;
                              learn again
that Aurangzeb was cruel,
                              Jehangir
like his father before him, loved
the arts but wasn't so good at statecraft
which he left to his wife.

We have ten miles to go
when I decide
I don't want to go back to America
or to change the fabric
of my first body.
                              Tonight
I want to sleep with a man
raised on dahl and rice.

---

[11] Major city in Odisha/Orissa

But at five miles to go
we pass a man digging
a small trench by his house . . .

and I see you,
my Yankee
                        on your knees
behind over the furrows,
scattering bonemeal for tulips,
your Dutch hands sifting the coarse dirt,
and I swear to you,
my one rose in the enemy dust,

co-heretic of love
defender of the faith
                        the human woman needs,
I will be back.

Main Street

Just outside the entrance
to Lord Jagganath's Temple,
I bought us each bridal crowns
and considered mailing them to you
in an envelope sealed with rice paste.

But I was afraid the postal stamp would crush
the sequined lovebirds embossed
in green and red, or flatten
the jeweled pillow;
                  feathers
would fall anywhere,
over three continents, two oceans,
two deserts and two seas;
the Sahara be hidden under
the belly of a pigeon.
                Imagine it.

               Over Africa,
over its small or great cities;
light meteors of sequins,
tinsel comets plunging
                into the Mediterranean.
             And on the savannahs
working men would stop
and unafraid
            stare at the sky,
and women
         on the way to market,
lay down their baskets filled
with copra and red chillies,
                  to look up
in amazement.

Villanelle

The nights are too brief for a life's long debt.
Till sundry griefs follow a sweeter phrase,
love, lay no claims upon me yet.

The earth's dark voice is not to forget.
I have dusk of faces and untenable ways.
The nights are too brief for a life's long debt.

until pause of lips on the winged fret
quickens owning of what the mind delays,
love lay no claim upon me yet.

Perhaps upon a time two Pole stars met
and a man's black curse was one to praise,
The nights are too brief for a life's long debt.

Those stars are unbegotten but I have kept
a brown palm open and my constant gaze.
Love lay no claim upon me yet.

Give me a matrix that a life may set
or leave light untouched by a roving gaze.
The nights are too brief for a life's long debt.
Love, lay no claims upon me yet.

First Mail: Delhi to Rochester

"I don't think migration . . .
necessarily leads to rootlessness. What it can
lead to is a kind of multiple rooting. :

What I have had is a feeling of overcrowding.
. . . too many voices speaking at the same times."
                    -Salman Rushdie, *NYT* 13/11/83

1

On the first morning—
at five o'clock
I watched the sunrise,
a damp rose
sweep the sparrows off
the scaffolding.

The Park gleamed like jade.
A Sikh jogged around the mausoleum.
An old Brahmin skipped rope by the bougainvilleas.

It is not right for a woman to be alone
by these salmon-coloured stones,
protected by nothing more than a star
made of two triangles.
But I have my notebook and my glasses.

*

I moved from arch to arch—
a place looking for a name,

or a name looking for a door
to fix itself to.
There's nothing else to
these spare stones;
no scrolls or jubilant angels,
no signs of saints or prophets to advise
a nameless governor.

I grazed through
the gradual swirling archways made
to receive the soul
                    gradually, disengaging itself
towards paradise.

2

A ten year old offers to guide me up
the narrow staircase winding to the top.
Gingerly, we climb,
our hands and backs against the walls.
He asks me where I'm from,
what I do,
am I a believer?

His slender hands curve—
wrenches perfectly designed,
the hands of Azrael.

Grandly I begin to say,
  "I am a Christian
from Hindusthan[12]."

---

[12] Hindustan is one of the names of India in Hindi

But the stairs are too steep
for drama, so I fall silent until
we reach the top,
                     and under the open sky
begin all over:
                     "I am from America and
from Orissa, from England and
from Ireland.
When I was ten
I lived in Delhi on Akbar road,
near Nehru's house.
In those days
a dollar was worth 4.78 rupees."

He looks a little puzzled then unimpressed
he shrugs until I give him
a bright, new one dollar bill.
His eyes shine.
    "I know how
to get fifteen for this."
Then he saunters off
as if he doesn't care and waits
to show me down.

3

Refusing taxis, fruits and lilies from vendors,
I wandered aimlessly around the city.

The language comes slowly alive,
My tongue
is henna-coloured from chewing paan,
At the post office,
        three young clerks

solicitous, friendly, explain
the postal rates in Hindi.
Grateful, I don't let on
   they speak too fast,
and make a mental note to commend them
to the Government of India Tourist Bureau,
to the Director of Telegraph and Postal Services.
They give me a receipt and I sail out,
happy, confident.

      As woman steps out of a taxi,
her magenta petticoat flashes.
It is the colour of my first sari.
I follow her until she disappears
into a jewelry store.
              There are armed guards
by the door.
          In a tea shop I settle down
to record my purchases:

The Biography of Babar: Rs. 100
Assorted pamphlets of the Communist
parties of Bengal: Rs. 55
Stamps: I am mortified.
            I am 56 rupees short.

4

On Akbar Road

the economics student takes me about
the house and garden.
          He asks
so many questions.

Oh America! Oh Freedom and Girls!
"And here was the gooseberry patch," I say,
"And here was the sweet pea bed,
and here the phlox.
Here is where we met
for prayers each morning,
and here my mother ate breakfast."

I rambled on about cricket on the lawn
and how, in late summer afternoons,
it glittered with millions of tiny fish
sucked into the pipes from the river.
                                                    They must
have died in the long dark trip
before the hoses spewed them out
on to the grass. My brother and I
looked for one that somehow stayed alive,
We'd throw some into a jar of water,
to see if the strongest, back in the mercy of
water
would twitch, a gill, a fin.
                                        None did.

And how fearlessly
we slept at night outside,
fighting or singing in the dark.
The air was an attar of grass and sweet decay,
and the stars, shimmering, silver,
swam over us as we slept.

Puri, April 1977

There's nothing between the ocean and me
but half-way, the bronze-gray back
of a statue staring out
at the same sea.

I know that frail back,
that large head, like a black sun looming
huge on the horizon.

My eyes focus and re-focus from my work
to the top of his head. I try looking over
his shoulders; to share the same vision,
its emptiness, its range.

    One small boat—
its sails like the voice box of a gramophone—
wings by. Yesterday
it seemed that the statue
had a twin and for a moment
I couldn't tell which was which
until one moved.

A small boy tried to balance himself
on the slight bronze shoulders while around him
a group of children screamed and clapped their
hands.

I don't know when
the father of my country
last served a better purpose.

Sand

To reach the water,
I scrape through a fence
of drying palms and sisal; pass
a sapling orchard bound
by salt-burned casuarinas.

Last night I tried to write . . .
to stop the fretful heart
shuddering at the least sound
of lizards and whirring.
I could hear it going
hard and strong
against the sound of waves
and the wind which never dies
in Puri.
Half in, half out
of water I watch the frail rafts—
fishermen mending nets.
Pieces of boats lie on their sides.

A boy's limbs sparkle—

                 flecked glass—

as he hauls in a boat
and helps his father spill
the net on to the beach.

A few of us gather
     as if
around a table of sand to chat
and weigh the portion in our eyes:
a crab with one claw,
one pomfret,

one mackerel,
  and quietest of all,
a baby dolphin
  stunned,
his tail stiff, pointing skyward,
one eye open,
I touch it gently
and smell my fingers; think
of the scent the man takes with him
when he lies with his woman at night.

The boy stares at me
and flushing, I back off,
return to my desk,
to dream under the whirring fans,
and listen for the heart
                        going strong,
skimming the waves.

Father

".. . the senseless asking for water."
                              -Kafka, Letter to his Father

Father,
in the night I ask for water,
not because I'm thirsty, but to test you.

I have wells, ponds and lakes
in three countries.
Lilies may not grow in them,
many fish have already died
but the pipes never fail.

Please give me water, then
I will go looking to my lonely work.

The First Thunderstorm

I wait for the thunderstorm to break
as I wait for a man.
The storm is sure to come
but I'm not so sure of the man.

The sky blackens.
There is thunder in the distance
and the crazed birds look for shelter.

A gust of wind lifts
my nightgown and drops it gently
over the parapet.
I chase after it,
and further into the rain—
the storm's eye—
for that second
of mutual recognition.

There is Only One Tribe

1

White gloved hands reach in,
so far in,
   the heart revolving
on its axis, can be torn out,
be crushed like a handkerchief,
or flutter
              like a flag
in a man's fist.

The doctors are always surprised.
Why are you crying?
Does it hurt?
          For sure
there are worse things I've known.
In my life . . .
in all its unladen spaces
new cargoes sound the grayest depths
until fluke and crown grapple
the one truest homeland.

There is no form by which I
can desert this world.
And though to be silent and
                to speak
amount to nothing equally,
I choose to speak . . .

2

Of what are you made America?

This April morning with
                        the yellow primroses
                        sparkling,
                        the rain light,
was it truly a woman who dropped in to say,
"I'm off to South Africa and know
what to pack from watching
the riots on TV"?
                        She laughs
and her laugh is shrill.
"Everyone is in T-shirts.
They're either too poor or it's hot down there."
And tell me why America,
a Brighton schoolgirl can commiserate
with her hostess
      but not the maid
caught fondling the lace curtains
and sighing, without guilt or shame,
"One day, these will be mine."

Does she resemble a Bantu girl
who may be strong in Scripture
and cross stitch—
which won't get her to Witwatersrand
to study medicine,
or to London
for economics,
or to Harvard for corporate law ?

Or was she a school girl such
as even I was
some 35 years ago,
a little up and way east of Durban,
assured of heaven and my heart's whiteness
by none greater than William Blake,
whom I still love and those others -
philosophers, poets, adventurers,
missionaries, painters, pirates, saints, etc.
who scorned my people
and knew nothing of our ways ?

Will this American girl become
a woman even as I am,
malformed, with the bones of a minnow
and an elephant's memory? . . ..

Let me remember the maid.
A Xhosa girl?—
In a garden of her own . . ..
filled with all the flowers
her country has given the world . . .
ericas, plumbago, gerberas
below a window of her own,
waving . . .
America . . ..

3

Years ago, in buried *The New York Times*,
a story of how a tryst ended
one night in Johannesburg—
a city of orange blossoms and bougainvilleas,

where the sun always shines
on cool, white-washed houses . . .

—of a black girl dragged out of a car
and taken to a hospital,
her male companion scolded and sent home.

Did she wish that she'd never been born
or that she'd died when she was young?

If it is possible for you to know
human fear America
pray the ballast
in the hearts of the poor
is purest mercy—God's.

Covenant

First he called from London.
Her hands shook. she began to cry
and was ashamed. But then,
she laughed too, because it was fall,
and even though outside the windows,
the air, things seemed to shiver,
the sun shone on. She put a red
silk dahlia in her hair and thought,
the ways of Allah really are wonderful.

Then he called from D.C. "I'll try
to come on Saturday. I'll ring again."

"Don't tie up the phone," she said,
to her household, and danced around her husband
and hugged both her sons and explained,
"He sent me out with hope
from India a hundred years ago, and well,
I owe him this and I owe him that,
and I owe him an airline ticket."

There were many calls that week but he
did not call. One Saturday came and went,

and then another. She took the silly
flower out of her black hair.
On Sunday night she said,
"Don't tie up the phone.
I'm expecting a call from God."
Now she's just sad
like everybody else.

Wisteria
for Ingrid Hall

May my crooked tree wisteria—
floribunda longissima alba,
bloom forever;
its pure white panicles shiver
always, always as mists
that can't be still.

Its perfume drives the finches
and English sparrows mad.
They chase through the delicate
branches and flit in and out,
in and out. Remember Waheeda Rehman
in a black *burkha*, standing tip-toe,

her head darting this way and that,
this way and that?
And those blazing eyes
when she lifts the gauzy naqab
all the better to see the ruckus
in the market square?

I forget what that was all about
but the hero saw her for a moment
alright, and so began a story . . .
and mine . . . At sixteen, publically
a tomboy, in secret I practiced
the *flashing eye* and *veil lift/*

let-fall techniques. I wanted
a black *burkha* in my wardrobe . . .
a good Christian girl like me.

But dear God,
that was an ancient movie.
I'm in the USA . . ..
My tree is white.
In my twisted life
shall I pluck it out?
I'm some kind of believer,

but no girl.

Anton & Marie Lewandowski[13]

Grandfather handled steel as
roller-man in the Tonawanda mills,
introduced my father to the men on his shift
"This is my youngest son Stanley"
& gave him a quarter to bring a pail
of beer from the corner tavern
to wash down their tin box lunches.
I only remember him
as a slight man in skivvies,
rumors of his long dying &
my father coming back to the car—
face gone pale, blue eyes set.
But memory can only affirm the past
& I want no such affirmation.
I know my life flows,
I can no more bring you to life again
than I could calm my fear of your wife,
Marie my grandmother, who spoke Polish
too loud, too quick, would grab at me.
She was crying; she wanted to hold
her grand-child to her breast.
Blood of her blood. Blood of my blood.
What caused that shrinking?
I was raised in another place,
another time, among cold people.
Coolness haunts me grandmother. Cure me,
Hold me, When was the last time I saw you?
Blood whispers through my dreams.
It has a life of its own, which I ask
my share of. Speak to me, my heart.
I'll understand where the words come from.

---

[13] A young interracial couple whom Hendrik de Leeuw and
Shreela Ray had befriended

Lesson

From the platform at Maritzburg
the train pulls out. The entire sky
embraces the smoke of its engine.
For a few hours Natal is in darkness.

All night a man stands shivering
with his luggage strewn at his feet.
His first class ticket would have been
no good even if he had missed the train.

Gray clouds over the city,
how in his heart did he spin
the fine cloth of forgiveness?

poiēma

for William Meredith

1

The Russian olive tree is dead.
All year its roots battled the maple's
and lost. I put it where I could see
it grow. Each doing its own thing
we would grow old together.

Today a silver heaviness is in my blood.
Gray leaves flutter,
gnarled trunks heave upwards to join
other things I have taken in
that are frail and cry,
which we run from or starve
the old, rain, desire.

2

This morning I read about Sartre's last days
of Simone de Beauvoir in the hospital room
with his corpse.
She wanted to be alone with him;
to lie beside him under the sheets.
"No,' the nurse said, "the gangrene."
So she lay beside him on the sheets instead.

I have often been duped by the fragrance of death—
narcissus, gladioli—unmasked now
as love's true opposite;
its fraternal twin, monstrously continent
and strong against friendship, blood, ambition,
and—most fragile of all—desire.

In her small frame,
in her old age,
in her eyes so
much defiance struggling
for air . . ..
              In the undertow, to think—

(given their faith:
without heaven and hell,
without God and Spinoza,
without pre-life and post-life,
sans change, sans magic, sans mercy,
or child of their loins to tell,
"My mother Simone, my father Jean Paul . . ..")

La mort so absolute, all
that remains is to make
all of the hour and place in 1929;
all of a terrace at the Luxembourg Gardens
where she first saw Jean Paul
strolling beside the lake.
             And if

there is room or need,
for blessing or for praise
to praise then her mourning dress,
the hands of the labourers who made
the window at the Sorbonne
where they first spoke; his first gift,
a drawing—'Leibniz bathing with the Monads'.

Praise to Leibniz in August
and that sunlit corridor—the tiny
existences alone, to make,
                complete a life . . ..

Snow Buddha
for my mother

The white moon will flutter and fall.
My exquisite and frail mother dies
with a smile on her lips stopped
by a snowdrift and her left palm
open like a leaf on her knee;
her right hand raised up. When these

castrated mavericks knock with their
comfort I must learn to say
it does not avail, it does not please.
After all these years I learn
that the brown sparrow cooped
in dazzling america complains
of the winter and in spring the green
rubs off like paint. And all night long I watch
the bright anger in her bird eye freeze,
and this alone avails and it does please.

Jericho

Jericho, Jericho,
how many of your
citizens lived to tell
what happened on that seventh day?

Who was the last
among you to see the face
of Joshua shining in the light
of his God?

Tell me this for I
was among the first to die,
and did not know why
we were fighting.

At a Visit to a Church

Birds in the ivy
below the eaves
busily usher in the evening
driftings through the window
the leaves fall. The leaves thunder

it is late. It is silence.
The virgin there
wears her title like a gilt carcanet.
She would not think she had it lightly.

In the wax painless face
used to being beautiful
the sunbeam catches the smirk.
There is a lesson in it somewhere. Is there?

It is silent. It is lateness.
As if the crafty
fiend always by
tapped me on the knuckles
I tiptoe out to where the wind

is fresh of my mother's hands.

Bodhisattva

Count me among the believers.

When I found you
the highway before you
was narrow and straight.

The sun,
resplendent through your body . . .
and the moon, a pearl,
spoke at your shoulder.
Believe her. Believe her.

There is much I will answer for,
but not everything . . ..
I cut myself off from my countrymen.
From New York to Missouri
I had pawned all of my jewelry.
Now all the money is gone.

Why did you stop?
Who told you that I
had run out of the pure water
with which I had come . . ..

How lovely are the flowers
you bring to my table.
But now even their radiance
cannot stop me from digging my grave.

Public Knowledge

Owl-eyed like Athena, secret with life,
She stirs me, beside me, at the fire.
Her black hair is rivery with small points of light
All around her face, rich corolla.
She speaks of green jewels. The fire sings behind.
Sweet smoke circles from her magenta cigarette,
Her gestures distending the night.

With this image I am caught back by reverie to a moment.
Naked, she is standing at a window alone
While the night wind roars beyond the pane
Galvanic in the trees. Within the room, moonlight.
It covers her bed and her lover with a glory.
He is staring at the ceiling. I know him. Gone.
And I know this secret in her life.

Yet I find I am smiling, for memory has discovered
In the shape of hope before a fire kneeling
Naked, myself, light in my hair,
Lover, in reverie, staring at my body
From the dark bed. And across this room.
Lovers, unless we lie. It is public knowledge,
And will be, again.

"I sing because I love to sing."

So began each singing lesson, near
the highest mountains of the world—
where I first learned to sing—
and innocently sing, ribald Herrick
on Schubert's catchy tunes . . .
Of Chloe and Phyllis
and falalalalas in roundelays.
A Latin mass was worth my soul
I thought, or could exorcise
ambition from the cradle;
but it did not.
                    Still,
with full voice, if not belief
I sang without a scratch or cough,
and let the mists over the terrai,
dancing up the terraced hills of tea,
bring home the Angelic Doctor's rhymes . . ..

Et antiquum documentum
Novo cedat ritui:
Praestet fides supplementum
Sensuum defectui.

In singing no harm ever came to me.

2

Our teacher was an Irish nun
called Mother Canice . . . already old,
blue, blue eyes and stately tall.
If you found her by chance outdoors,

in other rooms or the corridors,
she'd nod and smile and then,
as if lifted by a shy breeze
known only to her, she'd drift leeward
head slightly bent, eyes downcast . . .
Her long black skirt go . . . swoosh!
and she'd be gone.

We sing because we love to sing,
she'd make us say in unison.
We thought it rather silly then
but said it just the same
because she was our guru,
and although sometimes I did
not like her for she spoke
no language of our own,
and knew little about our music—
sacred or profane . . .
I never doubted
that she knew her stuff,
and from our pagan throats would coax
some of the wildest songs
and chants of the Western World.

She herself
was the wildest of all
when high in the choir loft
her pale hands flew,
like God-crazed creatures over
the keys of the great pipe organ . . .
her face in a beatific grin . . .
her veil tossing in the rose
Himalayan light at dusk . . ..
That same light and song blinding me,

we sang and sang out
to the hills:

Lo! Oe'r ancient forms departing
newer rites of grace prevail;
faith for all defects supplying
where the feeble sense fail.

3

Now Canice Flannery
to your shy ghost,

I, an old pupil send
my broken and orphaned dove
to say
        that the words
you made me once declaim
seem not so silly after all.

And I ask . . .
        as the last doors
of this land close on me
how will I restore my blindness?
How my sweet bird's broken wing?

I have only enough breath to turn the page.
Who will sing alto in my place?

SELECTED
LETTERS

Note:

What follows is a small selection of the copious letters Shreela wrote, of which she kept copies.

We kept Shreela's British dating convention (day/month/year), spelling and her own idiosyncratic punctuation, capitalization, and grammatical expressions which often diverge from standard use. We only corrected what seemed like obvious typographical errors. Shreela typed her letters, but often signed her name at the end in ink.

On some few occasions, we included letters written *to* Shreela, including a few from William Meredith, an exchange with staff from her publisher and Joan Cunliffe from the National Book Foundation, as well as an exchange with Noam Chomsky.

We conclude the section with a transcription that Hendrik De Leeuw made of two brief notes Shreela wrote while in the hospital at the end of her life.

Bread Loaf School of English,
Bread Loaf Rural Station
Middlebury, Vt.
2 August, '62

My dearest Miki,

Thank you so much for your long expected letter. You seem
to have been sort of unhappy when you wrote it, I think.
This girl you mentioned. I wish I was there to help you
figure out what went wrong and then I could have schemed
a way to clear things up. You know it is the boy who goes
to the girl first usually, but in this case, if you have tried to
approach her, and she continuously avoids you, it seems to
me quite clear that she is not interested and I do not think
that you should let it get you so very down. However, just
give her the benefit of the doubt and think that perhaps
she was having family problems or something similar. Time
really is the best solvent.

I was very sorry to hear that you did not do too well
in your last year and do hope that this year things will be
much better. You know I decided to write you a poem, but
I want to make it very good and then send it to you, but it
has to be so good as to be worthy of publication and you.
In all the stories I have written you have been in it as the
closest person to the main character in the story if it is a
girl. In fact my prize winning story is told with your name
as the brother, and from your imagined point of view. I
promise to send you a copy of the story.

What do the Fathers and the girls and nuns at L.C.D.
think of my success? Do write and let me know. Is Father
Abraham anywhere around yet? What about Fr. Coffey?
If there are any of the boys I know still there, please say
hello to them for me. I have become quite an expert on the

typewriter now, self taught, but my margins are uneven as the screw has slipped. I have finished another story here and am considering it for publication. I think that it is quite good and I may make some money on it.

This is a graduate college in what I am sure is the most beautiful state in this country. It is fairly backward, wild, wooded and wildflowered. On a hill and there are fields with tall grass everywhere. There are also many mountain streams to which I often go to cool my feet, and sometimes if it is deep enough, go swimming in. The college itself is very exclusively situated on this mountain, not really a mountain compared to the Himalayas, but truly lovely. The life here is very strange. There are about 300 people here altogether and the weirdest bunch imaginable, lesbians, homosexuals, married men and women carrying on, parties, some quite wild, and heaven knows what else. I have been in a lot of these parties, almost at the verge of getting drunk. It may sound braggish to tell you this, but I always have a crowd of male animals around me, which is sort of amusing and understandable at the same time, considering that I am the youngest, single hard to get girl, supposedly brilliant, witty and terribly mature. That really is awfully funny to me.

I have been told a dozen times that I am better looking than Sophia Loren and Lollobrigida. There are some faculty members here that have met Gina and think that I am. Gosh, does that make me feel vain. I am, if it is true, but deep down I know that I am not. People are afraid of me. Mr. Berryman, a friend of mine who is married and a brilliant man who was in India and lectured at Cuttack, said I should stop being so intelligent and sit back and just let people enjoy looking at me but that would be awfully boring. These things are always good to hear, but after a time are not enough, but they give me a peculiar childish pleasure. I

thank God for what he has given me and I regret that I do
not perhaps have the things that really count.

I am only taking two courses, one is Yeats and Joyce,
by Mr. Connelly, and the other is The Craft of Poetry by Mr.
Meredith. Both of those men are superb and well known
teachers. Mr. Meredith is a well known minor poet in this
country but he would be much better if he gave up teaching
and worked on his poetry. I like him a great deal, and he is
unmarried. Mr. Connelly is the most fascinating teacher I
have ever had and he is teaching the most difficult course
there could ever possibly be. We have finished Yeats, but are
now on the impossible Ulysses by Joyce. It is a monumental
book, difficult and challenging is not the word. As far as I
can tell it is the most impossible and greatest novel of the
century and possibly, one of the greatest in the world. Read
it some time but be careful, if you do not understand it, and
you will not unless you have a dozen other books around you
to always be referring to. You must know Catholic theology,
half a dozen languages, philosophy and every aspect of
human thought and activity. God what a feat that book is.

Since the courses are on the graduate level, I have to
work hard. I am at the verge of dropping the Yeats course on
credit, and instead just sit back and audit it. The exams are
this week, 3 hours each. I know that I will probably fail that
but Mr. Connelly told me to go on. The faculty sure likes
me a great deal. I get invited to all their parties and heaven
knows what else. This week end, I have been invited to
private party to be given for the faculty by Mr. Robert Frost.
I am very much honoured by it, having all this so soon. I
also was invited the other day by Mr. Meredith to a lunch
at which he wanted me to meet some friends of his. The
husband, Mr. Morrison, teaches at Harvard and is a writer,
I never knew this then and I was saying all these horrible
mistaken things I'm sure now, about Chaucer, and later on I

find out that he had done a translation of that poet. His wife takes care of Mr. Frost and I think that we will have a lot to talk about this week end because she is interested in flowers of Darjeeling, and both of us love Botany.

I have been smoking and drinking so much and sleeping so late, it is unbelievable. One night I almost ran into a little trouble when I was with a boy friend and we met some hoodlums, we escaped them though. Do not tell Bawa and Dine anything about that.

The day before I left St. Louis, I got $400 from someone in New York I do not know, it was anonymous and to this day I think it is the strangest thing that has ever happened to me. Almost like a fairy tale. I spent some money on clothes until I am now considered the best dressed girl in this area and Middlebury, really wild.

Middlebury is the closest town 12 miles away from here, and we drive down quite often to shop and get a few beers and drinks at the Inn and the bars. The Language schools are there and the students are not permitted to speak in any other language at all at any time except the one they are talking. You see them all over this old fashioned little New England town, at the bar and inn singing and talking in this language or that. You almost think that you are on the Continent again.

There are some very nice people here, the faculty and I get on well. Some of the boy students are very nice too. There are two in particular that I got to know very well. One of them I think will be a good American poet, David Laing. I try [not] to get involved with any one person really because at the end it is always hard to break any thing deep. There is no one here I could say, feels deeply for another one unless they have their wives or husbands with them here. Nearly all of them are teachers, I am the only undergraduate. My story, the Director of the college had told me and many other people, was the best thing he has seen in the Atlantic Contest ever. Once when I was terribly discouraged, he said to me that I should go on as I really have the talent, unusually clear in one so young, or something like it.

I have been getting A's for every poem that I have handed in, and one was very good, it seems. It was discussed in class with two other poems, but mine was discussed for two days, the comments were ruthless but generally very appreciated.

Pray for me very much. I have done some very bad things lately and am almost about to give up the faith. Too much I see that hurts, too much I feel that hurts. The most difficult thing for me here is to continue to live knowing that love is something that I can never have unless it be from my family.

I want you to do me a favour. Two years ago on the plane from New York to St. Louis I met a boy who was studying at St. Louis University called Pete McDonough. He is a brilliant student, very artistic and has done some very interesting things with his twin brother on amateur entertainment level with films, plays, and the rest. He is in the Peace Corps in Pakistan, and will probably visit India this October, if you get a chance to see him do, and help him all you can. He wrote to me up here, all of a sudden, somebody in St. Louis had written to him about me. I gave him our home address and he said that he will visit you all. I have to tell Dine and Bawa about it too, but just in case I do not at once, will you send them this part of the letter? Also he asked me that if I ever got to New York to see his parents for dinner and if I get to know him more, I might be able to see them. So do be nice. You might be able to drop him a line if I give you the address. Being far from home, I think that it may please him. He is about 24, mature and the rest, so be reasonable as you usually are.

Peter McDonough
Academy for Village Development—Peace Corps,
Comilla
E. Pakistan.

Another thing is this. Miki, if anything should
happen to me in this country within the next few months,
I want you to be understanding. No one will be to blame
except myself. Always pray for me, living or dead, you can
do more than I could ever for anyone, for Dine and Bawa
always my love. You need not speak about this to any one.
And do not worry, I just said this, in case.

If the school permits me, I will go to Rochester with
a girlfriend I made here until Webster[14] reopens, if not I
will go straight back when this is over on the 12th. So write
to me there as usual.

I have become a terrible correspondent and there are so
many letters that I owe desperately to people business letters
and the like. God will I ever get down to them and to my
studying. Tomorrow night a few of us are going on a drinking
party to the falls at about 11 o'clock at night, and we might
go swimming. The main reason I am going is because Mr.
Meredith is going and he asked me to go. We are both terribly
frightened of each other somehow, at least I am because I
know what could happen to me. He is about 43 and very
attractive in a strange way. Oh Miki, I can never reach him as
he is a very quiet and strange man. Oh I will be alright.

My darling roommate just came in with a can of
beer for me. She is a very wonderful girl. I'm really lucky
to have had her instead of some of the freaks I could have
had. She is young too unlike the others, and still very much
young at heart.

---

[14] Webster College, in suburban St. Louis, where Shreela was regularly
metriculated.

This letter better come to an end otherwise I will have to put 50 cents on it and that is quite a bit, although I understand that I owe this to you. I just washed and set my hair a few minutes before this letter was begun. Gosh that beer tastes good, it is Black Label and I prefer Budweiser, but now anything will do.

I am enclosing a picture of myself one of the boys took when I was coming out of my Yeats class. Notice the cigarette. So if you show it to Dine and Bawa, cut off or cover that part up. I think it is very good a picture, if not of me. I sent you a post card I think of some of the buildings here, did you get it? Write to me again soon and give me the news about Darjeeling. God what a country that was. When I get back to St. Louis I am going to see whether it will be possible for me to try getting a dual citizenship. Don't say anything about this yet, but I am going to try. I am determined to write and I think that I will be most able to do so here. That does not mean that I will not return to India, but I will stay in both. When I get back I will have to begin applying for fellowships to various colleges for my Masters, but don't say anything about this to anyone as yet either. Vermont has a lot of places where one can live and think that I would like to here, and I know full well that once I break into the literary scene in this country, I will be all right. I want to have enough poems and short stories to publish in a book before I can decide for sure. Must convince the critics here first. I do hope that will, it means everything to me. Pray, my own, pray for me. You cannot imagine what I feel and how easy for me it is to stop at everything right now. I can honestly tell you that I am afraid of nothing but myself and the future. Even death is not so terrible a thought any more. At least that means an eternal, tireless peace or nothingness.

Write to me soon. This letter will probably cost me 50 cents any way, so may as well go on and make it worth it. I just realized that I have no more cigarettes left though I bought a carton less than a week ago, and have already smoked myself penniless almost. I know this will mean cancer before 25, but that is exactly when I want to die, 26 better still but not 27 or any later. I guess I will have to walk down to the barn and get some.

I am really scared of the tests, you cannot imagine how much so. My poetry will be fine if I could be sure of the final poem I have to turn in with my criticism. The one I did write does not satisfy me anymore and I have tried and started three others but never finished them at all.

I will send you my poems, some of them and the one that was discussed. It is supposed to be like a poem of Frost's. I will enclose it here. You will have an idea of how much I have learnt again since I have been here, for the better as far as my writing goes, you will also notice that it is a style of poetry unfamiliar still in India to any great extent. Tell me what you think of it. I do not have it with me now, except for my own copy, as soon as I get it typed, I will send it to you.

Look after yourself ol' chap, and write soon,

Shreela

7/28/66

Summer Program in the
Humanities

My dear Dine Bawa and everybody,

It was so good to hear your voices. You came over very
clearly on my end. I was shouting loudly but was in too
public a place. My birthday was quiet and uneventful. I am
getting too old for so much fuss as in the old days.

How are you all, how have you been and up to? When
are you going to Japan? Or aren't you anymore? I heard from
Abu and he is fine. We hope to get together soon but very
little news from Miki. He has an irregular job at strange
hours but I hope everything else goes well with him.

This job is fun and simple although I have a lot of
papers to do. Most of the day I am left to myself. I have
been travelling a lot in the area and getting to see things
with the program. I take every other week-end off and go to
see friends in Boston or New York.

I heard from Ajay Appa. Uncle has a long trip to
S.E. Asia and Japan coming up on business. I will send
Miki all the money I can so do not worry. Babu tells me
that you are sending him $300. Have you done so as yet?
That would be of help and from there we can do the rest I
am sure. How are things at home? How was the wedding.
I wish I was there. Jhulu Mai sounds marvelous. I look
forward to seeing her.

The thing I wanted to ask you or to tell you, but
please don't panic because nothing is settled and I want
you to know this. There is a very lovely boy here 26, an
education major who wants to marry me and there is no
putting him off for a while at any rate. He has been very

good to me and I have enjoyed his company, also he is a good person and has been very good for my inner life and work. I told him I would write to see what you have to say. He is willing to live in India with me for the rest of my life. Please look upon this seriously because it has set me thinking and worrying and upset me in many ways.

These are the things I fear on my own part. First that for myself I do not believe in inter-racial marriage (but this has nothing to do with prejudice). 2) I want to return to India in time and make my living and writing there. (This is a complicated reason) 3) Family ties are much stronger in me than national, patriotic ties. I don't think I have the kind of courage required for saying to anyone from home "And this is my American husband." I am a social coward in such things. 4.) I am beginning to find openings in my work which is one of the most important things in my life (but he has been of some help here.) 5) (And this is most important and involved, I don't think I am ready for marriage, and am not sure that I ever will be. I am a lonely person, stubborn, reckless, inconsiderate often and I have fallen in love with my freedom in a sense, the pain the excitement of it. I have lived too long by myself to willingly think of sharing my life with another person so intimately. I like doing things my way, choosing alone, answering nobody, going and coming as I please. I know Babu knows this and respects it and a lot of people do. I am afraid that after a while I will miss my alone-ness. And last of all I am not sure that I love him enough.

As I said, he is a good, a good man. Babu will meet him one day. He has worked in camps in Europe and is now working as a director of one for retarded negro children. He has no father and his mother is very lovely and we get on well. They are an old, high class Williamsville family.

I am not asking you to say all right. I want to know what you think about this in general. I am so confused and the last thing I want to do is to hurt him. I know what it is like. I think he is very good for me, and if I don't love him in the crazy way I usually fall in love, maybe this is good, more mature and less romantic but more lasting, if respect and affection are there. God, that makes me sound old. I have prayed, as much as I do, about it and if I am worried now it is because the proposition is so real. Truly I cannot if I don't return to India but he is willing to return and work with me, he said he would write to Bawa himself but then I said no, let me first so that you won't be shocked. What shall I do, say? Anyway, there is time to think and oh, I know what I think is right inside but I won't say or do anything until I hear from you. Please Bawa, don't get too philosophical, and I would like Dine to write too and tell me. I can't treat this man like dirt, he is too good and generous but I can't as yet say anything. Besides I am too young, and yet I sometimes think how nice it would be to be married, children and all that, all my friends are but that is no good reason. One must be sure in oneself and that it is right all the way around but as always it involves risk, even the best, so-called wisest of relationships. Anyway, it would be easier for me to know what to do if I knew your feelings upon it. Now as I said, don't think that I am going to go ahead and do anything silly or without your knowledge and permission and blessing, not only marriage but any decision of such importance, but always, the last decision is mine. That is what is so frightening.

Well enough of that. My love to Rathnam and Joh and co.

How it is Padhi Uncle? My love to Bou and Koeli and all. I got Bugul's sweet card. I want some pictures of the chap. He sounded so grown up and authoritative. Ask his opinion, about the above. I love you all so much, I can't bear the thought of hurting you in any way. If there was just me, I would not worry so much. In a few weeks this job will be done and I will be in NYC for a few days before returning to Buffalo to fix an apartment. Write soon and take care. With all my love always. I will look up the man Bawa wrote and told me about. I hope I have his address and number. Would you send it again, although I think I have it here with me somewhere.

A letter from William Meredith
June 7th, 1974

Dear Shreela,

Because it will bespeak accurately my affection and
concern, I will reply the same day I have your letter. I am
distressed at what has befallen you, more because it seems
to have taken such a toll of your serenity and your sense of
yourself than because of the technical unfairness of it. Even
if what you take to be a satisfactory redress should come
about, the waste of spirit has taken place. I am truly sorry.
I feel your frustration as my own. I want to try to say things
to you that will give you a sense of your self sufficiency to
rise above this defeat, because unless the Human Rights
Division (of the State of New York?—you don't say) or the
ACLU can do something, I do not think anyone else can.
The Academy of American Poets has a small staff and 12
essentially mail-order chancellors, who conduct all their
business by mailed nominations and ballots, and their
whole business is awards: if they were to rise up as a man
and condemn the Rochester Board of Education, it would
not make a sound, that rising up. The National Endowment
people (and I spoke strongly for a grant for you in February
when I was a reader) are too political to involve themselves
with a non-citizen, or with an embattled citizen in most
cases. I don't belong to P.E.N., and of the three places you
speak of writing that is the most logical. But you would
have to draw up a much clearer indictment than you have
given me, if you wanted to enlist their help. You refer to a
CAPS grant, and I don't know what that is, and whether
the fact that it was never publicly announced means that it
too was denied you.

Another place in your letter that I'm unclear about says, 'John Logan says that I should go ahead and apply for the Pittsburgh anyway and also, if the ACLU does not take up the case and we decide to sell everything we have to hire a lawyer, some kind of benefit reading could be got.' What is to be applied for in Pittsburgh? Perhaps I could help there, and about selling everything you have to go to law: if the ACLU will not take it on, I think it would be a mistake to try it as a private person. It is this attitude, in fact, that I'd like to urge is not your own: you are being bent out of shape by an event which it may turn out you will do best to rise above. I mean it. Your letter lacks the wisdom and self-assurance that is what makes yourself and your poetry so beautiful. That's why I am so distressed for you, more at your response to this monstrous injustice than at the injustice itself.

You ask if your friends will give you moral support, and I can only say I will if I can find some appropriate way to do that, other than to write that Of course I stand behind you. I can think of nothing effectual to do until the ACLU or the Human Rights people have moved. Would it be appropriate, if they are not answering your letters, to go and see those people? There must be orderly processes and calendars and expectations for such complaints as yours. I would be very cool and orderly, but keep after them.

I will keep an ear open for jobs for the Fall. Now that I am back here I realize how tight the jobs situation really is: we have applications from more and better-qualified applicants than ever before. But I will recommend you above anyone else I know and there are a number of friends who need jobs just now.

It pleases me to hear of that good man Philip Booth being kind and helpful to you, but does not surprise. He would feel as I do the unfairness of what's happened to you.

You have every right to ask what you do in this letter, to become, as you flatteringly put it, a spiritual director. My regard for your work and for yourself, which I have borne witness to whenever I could, makes me want to do something now. But there is nothing to do about the Rochester job. From outside of Rochester, as far as I can see, I would be glad to write letters in support of your claims, or to come and testify about your ability as a teacher and as an artist. I will do that or anything else you think would be helpful.

At the same time, I am by temperament badly suited to support your response: I am proud in different ways; I would not give anyone the satisfaction of letting them change my philosophical stance. I feel yours has been changed without your recognizing that. 'Rochester for me has been an intellectual wasteland and socially a disaster,' you write. I find that self-pitying. I have never known people who complain about their locale who were not at some level dissatisfied with themselves in that locale. I am not defending Rochester, although I expect it could be defended, but saying that I find your response uncharacteristic of your true self—you are not a promiscuous complainer.

Write poems. Love your husband and child. Count your blessings, even though they are made bitter by this injustice. The publication of your poems is another thing, more a matter of bad luck than of any conspiracy. I have been trying to get two other friends published, Louis Cox and Helga Sandburg, and I know how arbitrary it seems to see some of the dismal stuff coming off good presses and not to be able to publish poems as good as your own. I can remember bitching a good deal myself in 1966 and '67 when I had been ten years unable to find a publisher for the manuscript that was at last called The Open Sea. I don't mind that you bitch, I mind that you capitulate, which is what bitterness comes down to.

It is graceless but not, I hope, ungenerous of me to write this way. I have had all the good luck where you have had bad, though at 32 my career was not a whole lot more promising than yours. But I want you to be true to yourself, and to keep things in proportion. Many women in America and most women in your own country, I expect, would consider you very lucky, being talented and not restrained by unsuccess from the exercise of your talent, being loved by a beautiful child and a fine man, being yourself full of grace and beauty. How can a principal and a personnel director of a school district reduce you to an almost paranoid distress? Don't let them. Put on your best sari and go for a walk among the beech trees with your two men and see yourself in the world's admiring eyes, then go home and write a poem. Not a bitter poem but an accurate one.

I would love to see you. But as soon as I get my desk cleared off I want to do some writing. My teaching has got so that it takes all my time during the year: am I getting clumsier at it? Do I realize more what it entails? I still like it but I need to be selfish about time during the summer, perhaps when Richard and I go to Stratford in August we could stop and see you. I will hold that thought.

Write again when you will—I can always find an hour for a visit with a dear and beautiful and valued friend like you, I would be a shabbier poet if I didn't.

Best to Hendrick and the boy,

love always,
Bill

Boston University
236 Bay State Road,
Boston, Massachusetts 02215
Department of English

November 18, 1975

Dear Shreela:

Hey! Congratulations! It's high time. I'm relieved. I
hope you'll tell Dustbooks to send me a catalogue or
advertisement or something. I was to buy the book.

I'd also like to write some useful brief statement for
the jacket. It is hard to know what I want to say, without
having the bulk of it in front of me again. That's because
jacket blurbs are topical and occasional things. The way I
would have phrased it in 1966 would have referred to ways
in which I felt 1966 needed the book. I mean, it's timeless,
but the readers are not. I've even got some of the poems
from then around, somewhere.

Look: even though I may lose it, if you have an
absolutely spare copy of some of the important parts of the
book, send them to me.

All Best.

Yours,
George Starbuck
GS:mh

Dustbooks
P.O. Box 1056, Paradise, California 95969

Dear Shreela,

We need to know some information which you may deem personal, but it is in a good cause. Are you an American citizen? Please let us know as soon as possible. The reason for this is that we have received requests for copies of NIGHT CONVERSATIONS WITH NONE OTHER to be sent to two judges reading for the National Book Award committee, Daniel Halpern and Theodore Weiss. I feel the need to caution you about getting too excited yet. We know several people to whom this has happened and nothing came of it, finally, but it is a possibility. The request form stipulates that the author must be an American Citizen, and we suddenly realized that we didn't know whether or not you were. We need to tell them this; the last thing we want to do is delay information or mislead the committee.

It is delightful to us that the book is getting this consideration. We nominated it because we thought it deserved it, but it's not often that the "prize givers" confirm one's own opinion. We both have learned never to count chickens even after they're hatched sometimes, because of too many years of hopes being raised and lowered at someone else's whim. But some good people are reading some good poetry, and we know they're going to be glad they did.

Please just a note to say yes or no about the citizenship as soon as possible. If you're not, they wouldn't give it to you anyway, and they would be angry if we didn't let them know. If you are, well, hope for the best, but don't place any bets.

Best,
Ellen Ferber

SHREELA RAY

One Park Avenue
New York, N. Y. 10016
Telephone 212-689-8920
Cable BOOKASSOC NEWYORK

October 26,1977

Dear Ms. Ferber:

It has just occurred to me that I did not respond to your
letter of August 10.
    Unfortunately, since Shreela Ray is a resident alien,
her book NIGHT CONVERSATIONS WITH NONE
OTHER, is ineligible.

    Sincerely yours,

    Joan Cunliffe, Staff Director
    National Book Awards

Ms. Ellen Ferber
Dustbooks
P.O. Box 1056
Paradise, Calif. 95969

209 Dartmouth Street
Rochester, New York
14607

29 November, 1977

Dear Ms. Cunliffe,

My publisher, Len Fulton of Dustbooks has informed me
of the decision made by your committee to disqualify Night
Conversations With None Other on the grounds that I, its
author, am not a US citizen.

Never during my association with Dustbooks did it
occur to me to mention my immigration status and I did
not foresee an occasion where it would be an issue. But
such occasion has arisen and I do here respectfully protest
the rule by which Night Conversations was denied equal
opportunity with other books of poetry considered for this
year's nominations.

You use the term, 'resident alien', whereas I would
and do use, 'permanent resident'. In any case, both are
terms conferred solely and properly by the Department of
Justice for Immigration and Naturalization.

I came to this country having just turned eighteen,
my college education is entirely American. My experiences
and my language are of this country and its people—a nation
of immigrants with whom I have spent seventeen years. I,
too, am an immigrant. Although I am not permitted to vote,
I pay taxes, and if I were a man, would have had to submit
to being drafted, in order to become a citizen, I would have
to repudiate the first seventeen years of my life and the
land in which I was born. I can no more do that than I can

repudiate these past seventeen years and the land in which I became an adult. It is this last factor which affected my decision to publish my first book in this country.

What I regret and protest most strongly however, is the injustice of this rule against a US publisher who chose to publish a manuscript in which he recognized a sensibility faithful to the 'American Experience' so as to warrant its being in the American Dust Series and to being submitted to you. Your awards and nominations are for a book already published by a US publisher, Night Conversations is copy-righted and published only in the United States. I, its author, am not a citizen, but the book is now the public domain of this nation and subject to its reviews. Your rule discriminates against the author, but most regrettably against the judgment of a US publisher who submitted to you a book, a manuscript of poems to which he gave the life of print.

209 Dartmouth Street
Rochester, New York
14607

29 November, 1977

Dear Bill,

Kay must have relayed my good news. I hope you are
pleased. I know it is not a BIG house of the east but
somehow my soul feels pure enough about that.

I am now scouting for people who could truthfully
offer me a line or two for the jacket. I hate those things
but apparently such things are necessary and it would be
helpful to the small press. I do not know what you think
about such things. I wish I could do it without them and
in fact publish anonymously. In any case, if it is not against
your principals and you feel you can give me a modest
line, even of good will and without alluding to my sex or
nationality, I would be grateful. If you agree to but need
more poems or the entire ms. I can send that, although you
may have enough already, that is if you can find them

The manuscript is called, Night Conversations with
None Other, is 85 pages long, with 46 poems written over
thirteen years. I must warn you that for that reason they
may be uneven, but I have been ruthless about pulling
things out.

Furthermore, John Logan is to write the
introduction, if he has not changed his mind. I have asked
Robert Hass, Isabella Gardner, George Starbuck and Mark
Strand for jacket comments also and anyone, or all may or
may not want to. But I think that covers a fairly wide range.
I mention this only in case it would help you to make
whatever decision. I mean you may not want your name

on the same page with anyone you can't stand. If however, all say something helpful towards the selling of the book, I would only include a few. More than three might be a little vulgar—like dropping names.

I have enclosed an envelope for your reply, whatever it is, I love you. At least wish me well—I know that without asking.

209 Dartmouth Street
Rochester, New York
14607

March 9, 1981

The Editor
Democrat & Chronicle
55 Exchange Street
Rochester, New York 14614

Dear Sir,

On March 8, you carried two letters castigating one of the few American leaders of Arab descent, Senator Abourezk[15], and Arabs in general. I am not an Arab—Muslim or Christian, and I am angered by the allegations made in both the letters. I heard Senator Abourezk speak at a diner to launch a nonmilitant but active association (not unlike anti-defamation leagues in their beginner aspects) designed to actively protest discriminatory and defamatory behaviour towards Arabs. At no time did he deride jews or accuse them of conspiracy.

If ethnic groups outside the ambiguous Judeo-Christian tradition may not protest racist stereotyping, cannot ask for equal justice, or disseminate information and points of view which can enrich opportunities for American citizens in making genuine choices over issues—then American democracy is a sham. To regard

---

[15] Of Lebanese descent, James Abourezk served as a Democrat from South Dakota in the House of Representatives from 1971-1973, and in the Senate from 1973-1979. Critical of US foreign policy in the Middle East, he is primarily remembered as the architect of several pieces of legislation protecting Native American family rights and political autonomy.

these actions as "anarchic" or as "foreign ideals infesting the American mainstream," is frighteningly xenophobic. This and the silence of so many Americans persuades me to believing that the current renaissance of the KKK and the American Nazi Party is merely a symptom of a deeper malaise.

Are Mr. Christiano and Ms. Cohen unaware of the prelude of racist laws, stereotyping, propaganda and laws connected by the Nazis?

Is Mrs. Cohen unaware that ethnic groups under the pretext of fleeing religious or political persecution pursue economic gain? This is neither new or wrong but "happiness" may have nothing to do with it. For many Arabs Palestine is their native land too.

Is it not possible to sympathize with the Israeli cause without having to resort to vilification and racism which only demean that cause?

209 Dartmouth Street
Rochester, New York
14607

14 July, 1982

Editor
Times-Union
55 Exchange Street
Rochester, New York, 14614

Dear Sir,

When the Nazis set about eliminating members of the
human race they thought undesirable, they did not do it
over night. The gas chambers and camps came at the end
of a long, steady, insidious campaign to discredit through
stereotypes the people who became victims in those death
camps. Years later, after covering Eichmann's trial, Hannah
Arendt examined how ordinarily evil manifests itself; how
thoughtless, without malice even, evil can be.

I am thinking these things now; I am writing these
things now, because I read in Mr. Taub's column about
the "harmless creative prank" staged during graduation
ceremonies at Monroe High School. A dean of students
mocks a Saudi Arabian chief and "buys" the school for a
paltry $2 million, (Mr. Begin on his last recent, short visit
raised $27 million). A school board member co-operates
in the haggling and the principal says that the school was
not defaced; this, from an educator—never mind that an
entire race has been defamed and at a time when thousands
of them, real Arabs are being really killed and really
losing their hoes a few thousand miles east of Rochester.
What ethnic group would or even should, tolerate such a
fundamentally racist "prank"?

I have a son at Monroe and I am a school teacher. What kind of education is he in fact going to receive under a system in which such incidents can occur so lightly. When Rochester City School can violate its own statement of philosophy and goals for "improved relations among all racial, religious, and economic groups leading to a more humane atmosphere . . ." how can it dare expect or ask for financial assistance from the State or City Council?

Sincerely,
Shreela Ray
Ph. 442-3003

209 Dartmouth Street
Rochester, New York
14607

6 May, 1989

Dear Dr. Chomsky,

About twelve years ago, as a small expression of my admiration, I sent you a book of poems. Please do not go looking for it, I have almost forgotten it myself so could not possibly quiz you now. This time I write independently to welcome you to Rochester. It had been my hope for many years, to be some day somewhere where you would be speaking, or in Boston to sit in on a class or lecture, if you would allow it. Or I would conspire and agitate to have you brought to town by some worthy organization to address the citizens of Rochester. This is indeed about to happen, and without any effort on my part. I am elated. For years I have imagined you sitting in my garden drinking fresh lemonade made from limes (as in India), rather than lemons, and attended by my sons. This is not likely to happen. The sun in Rochester cannot be trusted; one son will still be in college and the other does not yet care for linguists or politics. Besides, you will have much to do.

But there have been so many things I have wished to ask you over the years. None at all with any hostility, believe me. Perhaps you have answered them in some form and I have simply missed them or perhaps some of them will be covered in your lecture. For instance, I'm not at all certain that the Soviet presence in Afghanistan was unjustifiable considering early US activities in the Indian Ocean and subsequently the military build-up on Diego Garcia.[16]

---

[16] An island in the Indian Ocean, about 1,100 miles south-southwest of the southern tip of India, occupied as a military base by the UK.

The inhabitants forced to re-locate were never properly
compensated by Mrs. Thatcher's government as far as I know.
Before his fall, Bhutto was anxious to disengage Pakistan
from further entanglements on behalf of the rebels. If one
allows that the Afghan government was legitimate (I must
be persuaded that it was not), the Soviets cannot be wholly
faulted for taking opportunity of the invitation. For their own
sake however, I am relieved that they left.

Then there was the *Satanic Verses*, was it really a
free speech issue as the media made it out to be? While it
certainly made me think of things I had not hitherto thought
of, I was uncomfortable with the facileness and theatre in
much of the outrage expressed by intellectuals on both sides
of the Atlantic, Here it often seemed like an extension of a
personal war between the US on one hand, and Khomeini
and his Islam on the other.

But all this aside, I found myself asking,
hypothetically, for whom do I, a Third World writer (a role
and term I prefer to avoid) living in the West, write such
satire, and to what purpose? What I say in Rochester at
5 a.m. can reach Bombay by 5:15. Seventeen people died.
They are not famous. I do not know their names, their
ages, sex or professions. Does it matter whether they were
fanatics or sincere believers or merely bystanders? And I
have no power whatsoever in containing or defining the
nature of the response. These are sobering thoughts and
ought not they be so? The price of success and assimilation
seems inordinately high. Freedom of speech is a principle
I do indeed value but when I put it alongside values—
tolerance, self-restraint, of my other cultural tradition I
understood as if for the first time (Paul of Tarsus would
appreciate this) that these in their profoundest sense convey
freedom of speech without alienation, and I don't think
this is far removed from what Sartre had to say about moral
choice and individual responsibility.

Massachusetts Institute of Technology
20-D-219
Department of Linguistics and Philosophy
Cambridge, Massachusetts 02189

5/15/89

Dear Ms. Ray,

Just a quick note, in case I don't get to see you in Rochester
(I'm writing this before going, but it will be sent after
I return here, for reasons of hi tech too complicated to
explain—or even to understand). You're right about Diego
Garcia, but I don't see that that offers much justification
for the Russian invasion of Afghanistan. Millions of
Afghan corpses and refugees weren't responsible for what
happened on the island. About the legitimacy of the
Afghan government, I don't think even the Russians claim
that any more, at least very forcefully. As for the Rushdie
affair, there is, in my view, a very definite and clear free
speech issue. Nevertheless, I think it is easy to show—and
I've frequently spoken on this in public—that the sudden
concern for freedom of speech on the part of people who
manage to maintain their silence on very similar or even
worse cases nearer to home indicates that the turmoil is
more a matter of service to power and opportunism than of
devotion to principle.

You're right about the conflicts of principle. I don't
think it is crystal clear, but my own feeling is that freedom
of speech is something that we should value extremely
highly, and protect it with great dedication. Freedom
of speech issues arise precisely in the case of a message
considered offensive or horrendous; those are the cases in
which we must defend it, if we believe in the value at all—
and we should, we agree.

Hope to meet you in a couple of days—about a week before this letter will arrive.

Sincerely,

Noam Chomsky

7/11/90

Dear Dr. Lal,[17]

Thank you for your letter dated Oct. 27 which arrived
only a few days ago. Poor mailing services appear to exist
everywhere. The lovely stamps cheer one up a little though.
But how ghastly to have been so ill, and so far from home
as well. I hope you had some close relative or friends during
your incarceration and convalescence. Hospital and medical
bills are so outrageous here, so I am relieved to know
everything worked out for you. You are fortunate indeed.

Regarding DRAUPADI — I was under the
impression that you were going to get rid of what you had,
and when I saw you I only wanted 20 copies for sentimental
reasons. People are hardly clamouring at the doors for
my poetry, so I don't think another printing is warranted,
although it would be nice to get rid of those typos.
Ultimately I must say no. It would be too self-indulgent of
me, specially this time of year. But is kind of you to offer,
and I thank you regardless.

Sincerely,

Shreela Ray.

---

[17] Head/founder of the Calcutta Writers Workshop, which published
Ray's book *The Passion of Draupadi* in 1978; the book shares its
contents, slightly reordered, with *Night Conversations with None Other*,
and could be considered the Indian edition of that book published
under a different title.

16/11/90

My dear dear John,

At last I am writing to you again. I hope you and your
family are well. Are they? And your wife? I became
discouraged about writing to you, as to many others in
India because I was never sure that my letters were getting
through and it is important that I know this simple for
morale reasons. I have enclosed a form for a return letter.
What are your girls up to? Are they married? What are you
doing with yourself?

    The news about India here is depressing. Events in
Kashmir, Sri Lanka, the Punjab, and now the most recent
regarding the Muslim/Hindu clashes and the quotas for our
economically less fortunate disturb me. Please write and tell
me what you think upon these things. I miss you and India
very much. In a few years Hendrik will retire and we are
going to think about returning to India—at least to try for a
year or so. My youngest son Kabir, however, will be ready
to start college and depending where he wants to go we will
make our decision. Please pray for us so that may happen.
There is another big problem; please don't tell anyone, not
even Rathnam about this. I am in constant need of oxygen[18]
now and am hooked up to a machine that sucks in room
air, purifies it, there is a nose piece at the other end, so I
can walk about in the house and work. When I go out, I
carry a portable tank. I must find out whether the airlines
will provide me oxygen in transit, and whether I can find
such a machine in India. The machine runs on electricity,
so I will also need some sort of back-up system if we have a
power failure which as you know is quite common in India.

---

[18] Shreela suffered from sarcoidosis, an inflammation of the lungs,
that was, in her case, fatal.

Why did you not come to see me when I was there in '87? God knows whether I will see you all again at all. I hope God is merciful. John please forgive me for letting you all down. I should have brought Hendrik home. I still keep on believing it will happen. I didn't mean to stay, but Hendrik was too wonderful a man to let slip by. Hendrik was ready to return with me whenever I was, but I wanted to fulfill my own ambitions first. Please believe me. If you and Rathnam can believe this, and forgive me, my spirit will be a little peaceful.

But there is something I wish to ask you. When I die, I wonder if you and Rathnam take some of my poems, and translate them into Oriya and give them to the people in Paradeep and Cuttack and rent a car perhaps and read them through the streets down to the river. I'll make arrangements with Hendrik to send some money for this. Please do not tell any of my family about this. I want only to give them to the people I wanted most to honour. Honest to God, I don't care about anything else, and pray for me. I have a hard time as a Christian believing in God these days.

I wish my children could have met yours? Do they know English? Please write and ask them to write to me. I sent some jewelry for them last year around Christmas time but apparently the parcel was stolen. In fact no one got anything.

For the past two weeks I have been living in this little isolated cottage an hour away from Rochester. Hendrik will come to pick me up then to go back to Rochester. I have come here to be alone for two weeks. To have some time alone to think, read and write, and catch up with my letters. Won't you please write and tell me what you are thinking of these days? I am interested in your opinions about the political situation in India, and what do you think about events in the Mid-East. You know, I have never been trusting of US foreign Policy and I fear the worst had happened. We now have a fascist state even worse than Nazi Germany and I don't know what will happen to the poorer countries of Africa, Asia and the Arab world. I worry for the safety of our Islamic brothers and sisters everywhere. We must stop fighting with ourselves. Oh John, please write to me. I am so isolated and alone. I have enclosed an aerogramme for you to write to me with and a ten dollar bill for you to take your family to the cinema or something. Please let me know whether you get it and are able to cash it without any trouble.

My eldest son Gawain who is 21 years old, will finish his BA May '91. He is studying philosophy but doesn't know what he will do next. I wish I could afford to send him home to you and Rathnam. Hendrik is still teaching, 2nd std. He had bladder cancer two years ago, but now is perfectly fit, but needs to lose a lot of weight. I worry about this because his family has a record of heart trouble. My own problems I have already told you. Kabir, who is now 11 is a bright boy, but quite stubborn, and very much like me I'm afraid, but unlike me doesn't like books too much, and is very close to his father. I don't think I have been a good mother to them, and I hope they will forgive me. It seems that my whole life is one which needs forgiveness from many people.

I don't teach anymore not only because of my health, but because I wouldn't be able to find one even if I tried.

Please write and tell me where you live. Describe the house to me. Are you still a union man?

Miki is about 5 hrs. away by car. We don't see each other much. His wife doesn't like me, and I think Miki thinks he is my father or something, so once in a while we talk on the phone. Called him recently to ask how things were. His son Peter graduated this year from Harvard and has a job with Mitsubishi in New York City. The company will send him to Japan for 6 months too. He does plan to go on to graduate school at some point. Their daughter Lily still has a couple more years in Boston. I don't hear from Babu at all. He was going to come see us from Michigan with his 11 year old son Karunya but I did not want them to see me like this, so I gave them an excuse to not come.

Well, I will end now. Please give salams to your wife. She was so gracious to us when we visited. Take care dear friend, dear brother. And God keep you close.

affectionately,

17/11/90

My dear Jayanta[19] and Runu,

It has been a long time since I have heard from you and I am wondering whether I acknowledged your last letter or not sometime after Christmas. Perhaps it was just a post card. Anyway, here I am again to ask how you are and has your book at last appeared Jayanta? After months my book store gave up; but maybe I should try it again.

The Poetry Chronicle also solicited me for a subscription and contributions which of course I was happy to do but have only now gotten around to doing. No doubt you gave them my name, for which thank you. l am trying to discipline myself to organize my work and correspondence so I don't keep people in the dark or waiting so much. Towards that end, I have come to this isolated cottage just an hour away from Rochester in one of the grape growing regions of N.Y. The place is small but quite spacious inside. Large picture windows on three sides, overlooking a stream and rolling hills with a clearing in which yesterday I saw deer gambolling in the fresh snow. The snow has since melted and it was warm, dazzling and green except for the deciduous trees. I am absolutely alone, sans TV, but an excellent little library. The man who gave our writers organization this house[20] to be used for just such purposes as a place for rejuvenation and writing, was a history teacher so there are a lot of history books and reference works mostly on the occident, some rare works and much on regional flora and history.

---

[19] Jayanta Mahapatra, Indian poet, b. October 22, 1928, Cuttack, India.

[20] The Gell Retreat offers residencies for Rochester based writers to this day.

I brought tons of my own books but was foolish to do so
since I have been dipping into all kinds of things in this
library. The two weeks have gone far too quickly, but I
have made a great dent in my correspondence and vow
never to lag so much again. It makes me quite despondent.
Hendrik gave me this Panasonic word processor as a
belated birthday present. His name is 'beloved'. I have
not quite mastered him yet, so please be patient with my
errors. And hope that he will be a help.

I have not seen or heard from Babu for a long time.
He was planning to visit us with his son over the summer
but it was a bad time for us unfortunately.

Over Christmas I had sent some office type small
things and I think a small purse and kitchen item for
Runu. I am sorry they didn't get to you. If you know of
anyone who is coming and would let me know for how long
and give me an address I would love to try again just for the
magic of it, or if there is something specifically.

News about India is not good and I'm troubled then
of course there is this hideous build-up in the Middle-East.
Fascists everywhere must be rejoicing. I don't think any
power on earth at the moment can stop this insane country,
as my friend Bertrand Russell prophesied as early as 1924.
I have been trying to say so here and whenever I return
to India, but there I don't think people believe me either
because I'm a woman or an unconventional one, or is it
some sort of snobbery that I don't understand. Perhaps you
can explain this to me, next time when I come. Please write
to me when you have a moment. I hope you have been
well, both of you, and how is the writing coming? What is
happening in the seasons? I do miss them so, but a good
description would do somewhat. Not many people bother
replying to my letters or they simply do not get them,
which alarms me, and if it is true, I think it is on this side,

that is why I plead that even a post card acknowledgement
would help. I don't expect real long letters because I
know people work hard and it is hard to maintain a large
correspondence. So, I will close, with my best to you both.
And I almost forgot. The magazine containing my poems is
out, could you send me a copy? I have enclosed some money
which I hope will cover air mail postage.

So, take care,

cheers

14/1/91

Dear Max,

Thank you for the chocolates and then for the photos, &
the negative. I started this long before the war started,
and have been at it off and on. This is my very own [word
processor] I've named it 'beloved'. The 8 line display is its
only flaw.

You said something when you left in response to
something I had said, you said Nasser was ideologically
allied to the Nazis. And that you liked Mubarak and
Sadat. I do take issue to the first specially. To me Sadat
and Mub. are shahlike, prototypes; houseboy Arabs.
Mubarak is the highest recipient of US aid after Israel.
The price of his present alliance has been a cancellation
of his $5 billion debt. Public relations on their behalf
in this country has obviously been most successful. But
Nasser's 'nazi' ideological sympathy is a great surprise.
Could you tell me where I could find this information?!
Have been the semi-official resource for a local grass-roots
organization for their West Asia group. I know about the
Grand Mufti & Sadat's sympathies, although sympathy
may not be correct either. I have looked through all
my papers and books including his own Philosophy of
Liberation[21] but find nothing to ally him with the Nazis.
From my school days, Nasser, Tito, Sukarno as leaders
in the non-aligned group, and Lumumba, Nkrumah later
were heroes.

I have a biography on him by Jean Lacoutre,
published by Knopf, 1973 in translation from the French.

---

[21] Ray is likely referring to Gamal Abdel Nasser's book *Egypt's
Liberation: The Philosophy of the Revolution.*

Nowhere is evident the political or cultural philosophy
that inspired Nazi ideology. Nasser was in Afghanistan
for several years and did not return to Egypt until 1941.
Sadat however, and the Muslim Brotherhood had already
contacted the axis powers as did Indian Nationalists but
in their cases, it was not because they were ideologically
sympathetic but because they saw the axis powers as
enemies of their own enemies.

    The US has a version of history it wants to
disseminate, and it regularly passes disinformation to
'scholars' and members of the press, who naively may be
unaware that they are being used. The US has a consistent
policy of ignoring or humiliating TW leaders. Do you
remember when A. Dulles turned his back on Chou-en-
Lai's handshake? This recent letter to Saddam Hussein is
not unlike Truman's slap on the face to Nasser re. Aswan
Dam. The CIA tried to discredit A. Neto by spreading false
stories about his drinking and sex life. Who told you i.e,
of my having run around naked one night in Buffalo—and
other falsehoods? What would happen if I were to enter
politics in India, & friends here, even innocently gossiped
about me over a glass of beer?

    I've felt emotionally drained and exhausted. I have
come to see that very little from my pre Rochester past has
sustained me; that love and friendship cannot exist between
unequals. I blame myself for this & must do what I can to
regain some self-esteem, dignity which I've lost so hideously
in my life here. I had just turned 18 when I came I am
now 48. Very few from that life ever credited me with an
integrity or capacity for good. Except for the Hammonds
and Sylvesters & even there I believe I had to prove myself
over time. I think some think I'm simply making it up,
drama, you know, Roger Aplon, or Bob Hass, although I
did not speak of it when he was here? I know that the last

2 years have been ghastly for you, but I'm not speaking in regard to my illness only.
    The present horror we find ourselves in the Gulf is, entirely to be expected. Cassandra like, I've said so for years, & yes it is smug of me to say so. It is too horrible—it begins and it will end in the same injustice, I had prayed Europe would restrain the US. Only Islam and the Arabs if (they could get together) stand between the West and the rest of us, instead Iraq is alone and things are as bad as B. Russell predicted in 1922, the US as the most frightening military power the world has known, with its sense of mission and its cultural/pseudo-scientific racism will stop at nothing for world domination, this is not about oil only. It is about a monstrous appetite for power; it is about more bases in about the Indian Ocean, Asia and the Pacific, any little pretext in the name democracy for small corrupt rulers & US interests, about the need to humiliate, about bigotry of Judeo-Christian hatred of Islam, and the denial of the Arab country in Western civ. It is a contest, a struggle to the death against the non-European parvenu for the minds and bodies of the rest of us—that every head shall bow and every knee shall bend.
    You said you thought something good will come of this. I am perhaps stupid, but that horrifies me. The war had not even begun and you have already made the leap, anticipated good will come from suffering. As a Judeo-Christian I would have to say so but I am not. And I denounce and renounce it and fall back on my own less civilized Eastern values, and to Islam, that requires submission only to God, not suffering. I do not believe that good can come from such bloodshedding and warmongering. I don't want to live in such a world. I don't want any part of it. I wish I could go home. I feel unclean. For me to continue staying here is immoral. But I am trapped.

P.s. before I sign off, by coincidence on the radio yesterday evening, I heard the tail end on TV, Fred Halliday responding to someone complaining of S. Hussein with Nasser. Fred sounded quite forceful in his response; and most emphatically stated there can be no comparison, it is an insult to Nasser, he says & proceeds to explain etc. His work appears in The Nation & MG, and he is professor of international Studies at LSE. The capt. of the Vincennes was just honoured with a medal. Are things not up-side-down or is it just me?

but I remain fond

Shreela.

At least I don't say provocative things and then run.

209 Dartmouth Street
Rochester 14607

30/1/91

My dear Phyllis,

It has been ages since I called and we spoke. I don't recall
writing to thank you about connecting me to Dr.
Strider, who wrote me twice offering assistance and some useful
information. Things did come to a head with WM[22] but he
decided to give Richard a second chance it appears. I have
spoken to them both, and William is quite lucid. Richard
does not know I was making inquiries, so I feel quite
awkward addressing him at all. So it goes.

Thank you for your article on China. It all seems too
dreadful and I can't make things out. In India there are
young men and women who have grown up who have no
recollection of the Independence movement or how much
poorer India was even 20 years ago. Much like people here
who were born during the Vietnam War or the Civil Rights
movement. It seems hard for the older generation to give up
power although it may in fact even be paternalistic, loving
but deadly as we have seen many times. This kind is more
difficult to deal with I think than the violence of pure
malice, but I don't suppose it matters which kind it is to
those at the receiving end of it.

The present war[23] is too horrible and immoral. I find
the presence of French, Italian and English in a region
they once colonized in recent memory a special affront.
What is the New World Order to be? It does not look
promising to me. Who voted the US world leader? why do

---

[22] William Meredith.
[23] The Gulf War from August 1990 – February 1991.

we need one? Are we being attacked by another planet?
I am not a supporter of Saddam Hussein but I do think
things have gone out of proportion. Do you not think so?
And I am concerned for the Palestinians. I think it is over
for them and my conscience will never rest.

I hope you have been well. Send me things of yours
to read from time to time. I've written one little poem,
sort of godlessly religious and expect more such will come,
slowly. I wish I had the courage and energy to write on
other things. That may be the closest thing to salvation I
will ever know.

Teaching is taking its toll on Hendrik, which
worries me. Gawain will graduate from Oberlin in May, in
philosophy. He doesn't know what he wants to do from one
month to the next. Now he's thinking of divinity school.
Don't ask me where that came from, but I think he wants
the safety of a commune situation that is still mainstream.
He knows of my profound distaste for imported Eastern
religions.

I prefer them on home ground. He wants to go to
graduate school though.

We will still have Kabir with us for a few years more.
He is almost 12. I miss teaching, but can't do it. William's
new book should be out, called Poems are Hard to Read.
Anthony Hecht's new book is up for a NBA and is quite
dazzling although I am not comfortable with culturephiliac
poetry, but it's good. A friend gave me Wilbur's new and
selected works. I'm taking it in slowly. More to my taste.
Mmmm.

Everyone will be home soon, drop me a note when
you can. I do hope I shall see you this year.

love,
Shreela

14/2/91

My dear Kunti,

Do you mind my dropping the auntie? I'm too old to be calling you that. Besides, I may have acquired some wisdom along the way. My mother called a few days ago and told me that she had seen all of you. I hope she was not too much of a strain. How has your health been? I have been tempted to call you one of these fine mornings, and still may. My mother tells me that you have been receiving my cards and letters, which is a comfort, and that is why I am picking up the pen again. Hendrik gave me this word processor as a birthday present, recently and I have named it 'beloved'. It is gorgeous. Jazzy metal gray and quite wonderful except for its 7 line display which is not enough really for creating poetry or as clear as I would like, but I was in too much of a hurry to have one, so did not exchange it in the 30 day limit. Please forgive my poor typing.

At present we are all caught up in the terrible and unnecessary war in the Gulf. There have been large demonstrations against it all over the US but media coverage has been poor. The majority goes along with whatever their government tells them to. This is nothing new. But it isn't overwhelming. There are also many who feel helpless. I myself have become quite cynical and despair that the US is now the only superpower in the world its global ambitions can now go unchecked. Once I had hoped that Europe would try to restrain the US, but it is clear that Margaret Thatcher's England, including Labour, has been bought out. I still like Gorbachev but he has great troubles of his own. There is no one of the moral or intellectual caliber of Olaf Palme[24] or Sartre or Bertrand

---

[24] Olof Palme, anti-imperialist Prime Minister of Sweden, who was assassinated in 1986.

Russell to speak up for the rest of us. The US has got its own people in power in Italy & Spain, the only people who have stood up to Uncle Sam are the Arabs or "Islam," and unfortunately there, we have another set of tragic and complicated problems. You cannot begin to imagine the depth of ignorance and racial hatred this country is capable of, even in circles that should know better. Indians must never make the mistake of thinking they will be treated any better. I used to be a pacifist, but after living here, I am convinced that all the Nazis and fascists this country harboured after the war, have taken their toll in this country's psyche. The question of Israel/the Palestinians also has twisted justice and decency. That the rest of us suffer because of it, is irrelevant. I am very sorry to hear that India had permitted us planes/ships fueling stops. There are close to 6 million North Africans in Europe. Men who have messianic and racist philosophies hold powerful positions in both Europe, Israel and us. The spectre of genocide looks fresh. Since Bush has been in power, there have been 5 military interventions. I am sorry that I cannot be optimistic about this country in relation to Asia—the Third World in general. Many cannot bear the thought that India has survived; indeed more than survived without using the drastic measures of Chinese or Soviet models. I'm not one of those who thinks that socialism has failed; quite the contrary. I think it will go through many changes. There must be other ways of standing up to US bullying. Fascism is in full bloom so don't be fooled by clichés about democracy and all those silly Hitler metaphors; US self-descriptions actually. If you still have access to the Fulbright library, let me recommend a bi-monthly called the Nation. It is the oldest & greatest of American news journals; well written and researched on a great variety of subjects including the Arts.

A few days ago, we thought winter was over for but the snow is back and the chill. I have a white wisteria which I am training as a tree, but don't have the heart to cut it back when I should, so it is quite free forming. I have made many mistakes in plant selections. A plant chosen for its colour turns out to have large coarse leaves which take up way too much space in my small plot. Americans have not as yet discovered sweet peas, which I love but have had mixed success with because I never get the seeds in on time. I'm not physically able to do much lifting and carrying. Hendrik does a lot, but he has a bad back & I don't like him to do so much. We picked the wrong kind of garden for us. It's the kind that looks informal or English (why do they get credit for everything—but perhaps mine is a little anarchistic, me being Indian. In fact I'm quick to point out, it looks like an Indian miniature). But one has to labour hard to give that careless effect. Another friend has a formal Japanese style garden requiring little maintenance, once it has been laid. If I'd known I was going to be physically crippled at 45, I would have thought twice about the kind of garden to have. Still, gardening must be the highest form of civilized activity I know. The idea of actually taking a seed from one part of the world to another, of planning and design, colour and size for the end simply being for human pleasure. Does it redeem our bloodthirsty natures somewhat? Do you know that Saudi Arabia is a major producer of Rose attar and waters? And look: what they are up to now. If I had my life to live over, I think I would study horticulture. In fact, if I was healthy, I would do so now.

Hendrik is still teaching elementary grades, grade two but this year seems to be the worst. He has to work for 4 more years before he can think of retiring. We think of India, or at least giving it a try, but that idea has had something of a setback I will explain later. My oldest son, Gawain graduates with honours this June, in philosophy. I don't know what earthly use he is going to make with philosophy. I must give up my dream of a palace in Delhi and a summer cottage in Gopalpur. He is a good and gentle person like Hendrik and very patient. Right now he is playing with the idea of going to divinity school. I don't know how this happened since the state of my religious and spiritual life has taken quite a beating these 30 years and has never fully recovered. That is to be expected I suppose but there is nothing to replace or to equal that loss. But we do have love—friendships and family, relationships conducted over great distances that still tie me to this world, so of course I will make much of them. My youngest, Kabir, is quite different. He is in 6 grade.

I have written and completed one very long poem on the garden for Kabir, a few short stories but have not been sending them out. A few poems have appeared here and there, and I'm trying to put another book together. It's going very slowly.

How has your health been? And the V. Singhs? I will write to them too, but until then, please give them my best. What have you been doing? Do you still have your bridge group? I dream of seeing you again and to weed and putter in your garden, but as I recall you had no weeds and I remember your introducing me to the asoka trees. Something was wrong with them at that time and you were a little concerned. Perhaps there was a water shortage. Do you see Asha? My regards. She owes me several letters. Is she still with that man? Now I have to tell you about my health. I would not do so except that I cannot write to anyone in Orissa because whenever I have tried to give or ask for any information about anything, they panic or ignore my questions. They never respond, I have been very ill for the last six years and since January 1st 1990 have been in constant need of oxygen. The device they have here is called an Oxygen Concentrator. It takes in oxygen from room air and gives back the Carbon Dioxide. It runs on electricity. I am fully able to move around normally because I am connected to the machine by a 50 foot clear plastic tube which has a nose piece. When I go shopping or out socializing, I carry a portable tank which I fill up from a "mother" tank of liquid oxygen. I need to know whether such a device is available in India, and how much it would cost to rent or buy one outright. Perhaps there is an Indian-made version of this thing, and also a portable one that can carry me over from plane through airport-to-car-to-destination. I'm sure there must be such a thing, and a pulmonary specialist would know about this and "liquid" portable units. Unless I can get this, my returning to India is out of the question. I still have to find out whether any airline will let me carry a portable tank on with me and allow me to use their own oxygen at a reasonable price. Do you or the V. Singhs know a doctor friend or a hospital director who could give you this information? Please don't go researching this on foot over hill and dale. I'm hoping a phone call or two would be enough. If it is inconvenient, you must on no account bother. I will also be writing to the consul here. But without this I can't go back, and cannot go anywhere alone. I have only 20% heart/lung capacity. When you saw me last, the doctors here were not sure I could do it, but they also knew that it was psychologically important. I started out believing it was my last sight of India, and I was glad that you were part of it. But I'm greedy, and want more. I want to see you again, my mother and Ratnam. Do you remember him? He was our cook and our rock and refuge. I made a personal commitment to him and his family and myself, that I would take care of them.

That is the biggest guilt and shame I bear, and also for my youngest brother.

Among the many things I have thought about over the last few years as I struggled with my health, is that it is nonsense to say that there is a brain drain. I met many committed and brilliant hardworking young men and women during all of my visits home, and can assure you that not all of those I've met here, including myself are not always the crème de la crème but have had the means or contacts to leave India. Now more and more come, and many come from what sociologists would call 'lower' middle-class families. If to be able to 'go abroad' is a good thing, then naturally I am glad to see more Indians from other classes and in non-service or 'useful' fields studying abroad. On the other hand, I believe there is something wrong as long as we believe everything good to know, to learn, and to have is Western. Perhaps unintentionally we have colluded in the myth of our own inferiority. I don't mean to rekindle 'us' vs. 'them' postures—it's more complex than that, and I don't put any moral blame on anyone, but for me it has meant that for the last 30 years I have pretty much lived a lie. And I have come to ask myself—surely there are values of my own culture that deserve recognition specially when I live in a country constantly needing to wave the flag of West. civ. I found that the ideas of tolerance and compassion are surely great contributions of Eastern civ. even though we often find them in contradiction to manifest values; but not more so than Christian militancy against the concepts of faith hope and charity. I'm not a romanticist; quite the contrary. The impulse to save the world often ends in disaster for everybody. Learning to cut one's self down to size, to try to live a quiet decent life, and to just caring for those around one is no mean task.

Now that I am physically broken and old, I think of returning to India, hoping that if just that ("they also serve who only stand and wait' as Milton wrote), will cheer my old aunts, my old teachers, those who stayed on to work hard and kept India going rather well and in spite of all the terrible stress she has been under and continues to be, it will be worth it. The growth I saw between '77 and '87 was far greater than from '60 to '77. The material quality and quantity of change was beyond anything I had imagined. But that is not why I want to come home. The truth is, no matter how hard I may try to assimilate, I would remain a second class citizen. Naipaul's new book on India got good reviews here, and apparently he was quite pleased with what he saw and hopeful which is a far cry from his two earlier books on India. He is a great writer but I do have many difficulties with him. You?

A good friend and retired professor of mine whose daughter has married a Madrassi boy, spent 2 months there. Returning he said to me, "Everyone kept saying there was corruption everywhere and nothing gets done, but everywhere I looked things got done, or kept going. So what are they talking about?" I agreed with his point, but confess to a little unease with what appears to be a burgeoning of new temples and public displays of religiosity going hand in hand with the yuppieness & materialism. True?

What did you and your friends think of the Rushdie case?

In the US it was made into a free speech issue when it need not have been, but it also made me think about a lot of things I'd not thought of before because nothing like this has ever happened before in the history of mankind. Modern technology is such that what I assay at breakfast in Rochester can reach you for lunch, and along the way, anyone can change it to serve it differently.

Americans assume that everyone plays by or ought to play by their rules only. Rushdie did not understand how deeply humiliated and vindictive this ignorant and racist country is vis-à-vis the Iran hostage crisis, Arabs and Islam, the Third World. Generally, Rushdie is a brilliant but flawed writer, ambitious and competitive in the intellectual jet-set culture and would probably like to be the youngest to win the Nobel Prize. He needs to control his predilection for ironies and for showing-off his cosmopolitan erudition first. Some American publisher probably encouraged him at a fancy cocktail party, to put in the offending passages. I read somewhere it did indeed happen that way. (So did Gita Mehta's Karma Kola.) Things sort of boomeranged after that. The Europeans dealt with the situation much better, quietly and effectively. In New York we had the absurd and melodramatic spectacle of three Jewish writers giving a public reading of the offending passages. Someone asked me didn't I think them brave, and I said no. They are too famous, and stupid, and the fact they're all Jewish doesn't help. It further politicizes things insensitively.

Please drop me a line. Tell me what is growing in your garden. What does the February sky look like at dusk? Have you had anymore Oriya cooks? If I were fit I would offer my own services. Perhaps I should send you my son for a year, to make something useful out of him in your garden or kitchen and learn the language.

Is there some little thing I can send you from the American bazaar? When are you coming to visit? I'll look for the best bridge players in town and throw you a big party. No. Several little ones. Bring Viru and Mohini too. I hope their health has been good, and yours. When I saw you, you had recently come out of the hospital. Please drop me a note, What fruits are in season and flowers?

Kunti, please don't tell anyone in my family about my condition. The disease is called Sarcoidosis. It's chronic but not fatal 90% of the time, but my variety is the 10%. There is no cure for it but some can be treated for a while with steroids in the hope that the body will fight back. It is another one of those immune deficiency diseases. It severely limits my activities, but I can move around, cook, read and write.

So, once again, cheers, write.

love,

22/2/91

My dear Cornelius,

Thank you for the tape and poems. I have read the poems-
songs?- and am bowled over, but we haven't listened to
the tape yet. H. has been too sick to move intelligently
and listen, and I don't want to be knocked off the planet
entirely, but little by little.

How is the long distance marriage working? My love
to Sarah when next you speak. I'll drop her a note myself
in a few days.

I'm deeply shocked and saddened to hear about G.
Starbuck's having Alzheimer. (By the way, the very day of
your letter there was a news report that British Scientists
had found a defective gene the cause of Alz. I have not
seen any written news since but will keep my eyes alert.) I
owe George a great deal and was terribly fond of him and
I used to baby sit his children. I don't think his wife liked
me although she had no reason to worry. Upon arriving
in Buffalo I found that she had maligned me most cruelly.
His present wife Kathy, had been super competent dept.
secretary and I had liked her but years later, when he
came to read at U of R, she was awful. After the reading
I skipped down the aisle to say hello and embrace them,
but she looked at me silently and with such contempt,
I can't forget. George invited me to the party later, but
there was more of the same, and he was sort of guarded,
but promised they would stop on their way back to Boston
the next day after brunch with the Hechts. Hendrik,
Gawain and I scrubbed and cleaned the house like mad,
and waited and waited and waited. Gawain fell asleep, and
when he woke up the first thing he said was have they
come? They never came, or wrote or called. I felt like shit,

humiliated before my kid, and swore never to host an N. Amer. poet again. In my book, I refer to that incident in one of my long poems to Gawain.

I frequently think I would have been happier and more successful if I had gone south. This week Richard Harteis[25] berated me for expressing my disappointment that no one had thought to include me in festivities honouring him May 16. Having been an unusual protégé of his and friend, I thought no harm in expressing my hurt. Oh well.

My regards to George. He left a sad hole in my life, and I don't know what I did wrong. But that doesn't matter at the end. I am quite shaken and pray.

You sound happy. Do you mind if I send some of your poems to a musician friend of mine with a band in Boston? "Now you take care now yo heah?" But seriously, I hope you and Sarah take a complete physical regularly. Time to sign off. See you in March, and you know I'd love to have a party for you, but don't trust my health, but maybe with Leah. How does the book look? Nobel stuff?

love,

---

[25] William Meredith's partner.

25/2/91

My dear Padmalaya Appa,

How good it was to receive your letter, but how short and
without any news of yourself, your family. What are you
doing and how is your own health? I just received a letter
from Dei penned by Kisu. It seems it is difficult for her
to find anyone to do this since she can no longer see well
enough to write. I have frequently thought of calling but
have been deterred now by your news regarding theirs being
often out of order.

Hendrik and the boys are fine, except that Hendrik
is just recouping from an ugly flu and a bad back. His
schoolwork is not going well since he has a particularly
difficult group of 2nd. graders. For the first time since '72 I
am seeing him dread going to work. The war in the Gulf is
not helping his spirits. As you know, I have been trying to
tell people every time I have come home, that this country
has a dangerously fascistic ethos. Now that the cold war has
been declared over; the US. as the only super power left is
unstoppable, specially with its new alliance with Britain.
Bertrand Russell predicted as much as early as '22. Now
it is acting to destroy the only potential, dignified power
that could challenge it, the Arabs/Islam. I worry deeply
that India's present government will sell out by indulging
the US and thereby make even more fragile the lives of
our Muslim brothers and a sisters in our country. Dear
lady, believe me, this must not happen, and I pray that
India will not be duped into roles and alliances that will
indulge US insatiable appetite for power and humiliation.
They have never liked India much because we have stood
up to them in the past, and they are no less racist than
the Brits, but a little coarser and jingoistic. They gave

shelter to an extraordinary number of Nazi criminals in the US or found havens for them in Latin America. I think terrible things lie ahead of us because already the political scientists and 'experts' are speaking of Asia as the next 'theatre' for US activities and ambitions. I don't know what is going to happen to the Palestinians now. Europe has several millions of peoples from N. Africa and I don't doubt for a minute that the genocides practiced earlier in our century can happen again. Sometimes I wonder whether us practitioners of the older major religions (Hindu, Jud., Xian, Bud.) resent Islam because it was born relatively recently in a historic time-period universally accepted, and has a world-wide following and therefore the impudence to demand being taken seriously.

As a wayward, sometimes godless Christian with strong Hindu shadings, I find that demand attractive in our racist and bloody age.

I still have most of the bangles you gave me. They impress and delight everyone who goes into my bathroom where they are displayed on a little oak shelf with spindles that Hendrik made for me. Won't you come and see for yourself?

In my house I have a Champa tree which is surely at least seven years old, but it has never bloomed. Also an Oleander and a forlorn looking Jasmine which did rally enough last summer to give me two blossoms. Our winter drags on, one day snow melts, the next, freezes. This brings out the worst in most people. Marriages threaten to break-up or some threaten to throw themselves off a cliff somewhere. I am one of those in both categories, but yesterday Hendrik told me that he heard the Canada geese flying South, so I am happy again, or at least for the moment.

Before I sign off, I wonder if you could send me the names and addresses of journals or magazines that publish poetry that would be interested in my work. Hardest of all

is for me to tell you that it is unlikely that I will be able
to travel again to India. I would like to explain why to you
but need you to assure me that you will not speak of this to
anyone, or at least until I look into a few things. Could you
send me the address of Mrs. N. Satpathy.

How are things under the new PM? We hear reports
of communal riots? How extensive are they, and what about
Kashmir? Well I've come to the end. I will write again
soon, and hope to hear from you again. Please take care.

love,

209 Dartmouth Street
Rochester, New York 14607

21 March, 1991

Len Fulton
Dustbooks
P.O. Box EE Paradise, California 95969

Dear Mr. Fulton,

For several years now I have tried to reach you by phone
and through the mail and not once have you responded.
You cannot know what misery it has been, to be so cut off
from so many things as one gets older.

I thought at first that it was the NBA or Joe
Flaherty's debt to you, but when I spoke to your secretary
she seemed to know nothing about it or to have any
record of the issue. The only other thing I could imagine
is that perhaps the conservative right organized during
the Reagan years had succeeded in denying another
minor poet/teacher a forum. These are not healthy
thoughts and I try not to indulge them. In the mainline
political literature however, this wouldn't be far-fetched.
People are blackballed, even when they can't prove it and
there are so many seemingly harmless ways of silencing
people. But I cannot really believe it is the case here or
that you would be so gulled. Please tell me what then is
the matter?

You have not sent me any statement indicating how
sales of Night Conversations have been going for many
years. I don't expect royalties, but assume nonetheless that
an author would be routinely informed regarding such
matters. And naturally I am curious.

You have me in a hopeless situation because I can't do anything more than to plead that you tell me why you will not talk with me or write. There is something terrifyingly Kafkaesque about this. My health is completely shot, my will and energy low. I am cut off from work and travel, and have no legal or political clout; I cannot threaten you or behave against my nature, so please tell me why you have so deliberately shunned all my communications and not send me information on my book. There is nothing else I want from you.

Sincerely,

Shreela Ray

21/3/91

My dear Ranju,

Anna will give you one letter, and this one will probably reach you after that. How lucky you are to have me to shake up your life a bit. Earlier this month Rochester suffered a strange storm. An ice storm. The melting snow suddenly froze on the branches and turned this county into trees of glass. 90% of our trees broke under the weight and have damaged all of them severely. We were declared under emergency and out of electricity and telephones for almost two weeks. One or two houses on a block would have some power and others for part of the time. We slept in the living room in front of the fire and went to more fortunate friends for supper, where I could cook fabulous Indian meals for anyone who came. It was quite an adventure. Only one senior citizen unfortunately died, and she, from freezing. Otherwise people helped each other but complained a lot. It is evident that Americans cannot tolerate the slightest discomfort to their extravagant lifestyles. I was quite amused and thought it would have been a wonderful opportunity to tell ghost stories on the streets and barbecues on coal fires, sing, stage candlelight plays, hide-and-seek etc.

What have you been doing with yourself? This is my very own Word processor Hendrik gave it to me for my birthday last year and I love it dearly although I have not mastered it and my typing has always been poor. His name is 'beloved' and he is a handsome metallic gray and black Panasonic. The only flaw is its 8 line display. I wanted a 14-16 liner. Do they make such things or are they available in India and if so, for how much?

Ranju, I ache for India and am afraid that I shall never see her again. Never see my old aunts, my Ratnam. My mother, you, just the river, the dust. The cows, and eat raw mangos with salt and chilies and borr koli, akkhu badi. That I will never hear film songs blaring out of cars with loudspeakers affixed on top, a cricket match. Just the physical act of transporting me back is such a huge hurdle. I think God is punishing me for all the betrayals, the failure to go back, Hendrik, all my self-indulgence and waywardness deserve this. I cannot complain but the misery is great and it keeps growing and growing I often feel like giving up altogether because my ability to function and do all the many things I used to is severely curtailed. I have become reclusive and don't like being seen so handicapped, and having people want to help embarrasses me, so I stay home and see a handful of friends. I can't travel alone and so I cannot give anymore readings out of town. It is difficult for me to concentrate on things, even reading or sewing, and I am afraid to drive so have to rely on other people Hendrik does most of the food shopping, taking Kabir places. I barely manage to cook and we send out a lot. I have put on about 20 lbs., which is OK since I had been way too thin, but I am uncomfortable.

Mostly, I think Hendrik and my sons did not deserve this and I think the best thing for me is to get out of their lives. I seem only to have caused suffering in my life everywhere, by absenting myself from my loved ones in India and then helpless with those here. People are so kind to me, I cannot bear being with them because I feel obliged and want to do things for other people but can't. And the social and political issues that I care about, I don't have the energy to work for them.

Please write and tell me about India. Pretend that you are speaking to someone who has never been there. How does the day begin? Is it raining? What is it like when it doesn't rain. And what do you see or hear when you look out the window/don't tell me about the well-off Indians only. Tell me about the people who work for you in your own house; what are their names? Are they fat or thin? Do they have children? How many and where do they go to school? And what do they dream about? Tell them something nice about me. Tell your cook for instance that you had a friend once who went away to the US and is very unhappy and longs for Indian food such she/he would make and that if he would please give me a recipe, or you could write it for him—for brinjal or for an okra (lady's fingers/ bhendi) dish. The University of Rochester recently (in the last 5 years) created the William E. Simon school of Business Administration. It started off a little scandalously, but may be the only thing that will survive around his university. I just called to have them airmail a catalogue and application form to you. Let me know as soon as it arrives.

I'm sorry if my call created any strain and grief. What have you told your wife about me? She should have no cause to worry surely. You have not misled her I hope in regard to me. Of course who knows what life is like for men in your position in a country heavily favouring male privilege.

This letter will ripen over several days, so I will stop for now and start supper. Someone brought me some shad which is like our hilsa,[26] and it is the season for it.

1/4/91

Yesterday was Easter and I had a few friends over for paschal lamb dinner, which was quite superb if I say so myself. I had marinated it for 3 days in loads of garlic, fresh

---

[26] A type of freshwater fish commonly used to make fish curry on the subcontinent.

basil and wine as some Greeks do, or as I have been told. Our paying guest made an apple pie, and one of the guests a brinjal and mushroom dish. I like this very American custom of sharing dishes. Is this something we do in India these days? Do you have many servants? What is your home and house like? Describe it to me, and the view and the neighbourhood you live in so I can see something at least with the heart's eyes.

Today I awoke late and wasted much of the time trying the NY Times crossword puzzle, and just began to do last night's dishes. It is already 3 p.m. and everyone will be returning. Kabir has boy scouts at 7 so I will have to feed him soon. Tonight ham and mashed potatoes and asparagus which has begun to come in. Last week was full of Indian meals. I made an excellent sour eggplant and shrimp curry in a rich tomato-tamarind sauce. You simply have to come so can serve it up to you.

How is your health? Did you make contact with Anna? I earnestly hope so. I have already sent Nirmala a letter and should mail this to you today. Enclosed is some samples of what the rich and fashionable are wearing these days in the US golf world. I think of all sports, golf and American football have the ghastliest clothing.

It is gray, wet and begun snowing again. I am dying to work in my garden but it is way too cold for me and I have difficulty breathing.

I have a favour to ask. Do you think you could send me a Salim Ali book on Indian birds? I think there are several, but I want a small one, a light weight paperback if possible and also a set of Indian clay figures. I bought a set at the big Delhi gov. emporium in the children's toy dept. for Rs. 24 in '87. There were a doz. figures in various dresses about 2 inches tall, basically anything of that sort you can find would do and of Indian animals, street people etc. I think the emporiums would be best to try but you probably know someone who knows these things best. Would it be too much trouble for you? If it is, never mind; it is not crucial. I don't think they are expensive, and if they were I would not ask. Anna would probably not mind bringing them and one more thing and most important of all, some blank Indian postcards for sending out of India, i.e. overseas. I am assuming that they exist, or certainly they did once and I hope they still do, otherwise, aerogrammes will do so that when I send contributions, the editors can respond.

Did I tell you that I am a self-convert to Islam. By that I mean that as long as I live in the US and there are communal wars in India, but most specially because the viciously racist treatment by the US against Arabs and Islam I've decided to exist like a bee in the bonnet; to make them think, to startle them out of their smugness. I shall let you know how this goes from time to time. Last fall I attended a meeting to discuss how to deal with congressional threats to cut off funds for the arts because of some alleged misuse of funds for 'pornography'. I argued the devil's advocate in that taxpayer's money should not be so used and also what about blasphemy I being Muslim, what would happen. There was a gasp followed by a horrendous silence. These were college educated professionals mind you, and supposedly quite worldly.

I don't think that anyone had ever seen a Muslim in real life, and I was their first.

I hope this makes up a little for all my years. And don't forget to overlook my bad mistakes. I am very unhappy and miss India.

love,

22/3/91

Dear Sitakant,

How wonderful to receive your card. Do you know that over Christmas of '89 I sent you and Mr. M. a small package but it came back, partially after months and months and I could not get your new address from anyone.

What are you doing in Delhi? How are you and your family? Please give everyone my regards. I am sorry that I have not kept in better touch with you or done all the things I wished to for you. I think I have suffered a great crisis of confidence living here, not because I was incapable but because I allowed myself to be demoralized and the ensuing despair has quite overwhelmed me. America has won. I admit defeat, but what about our world? The Gulf war is only the beginning. US will go everywhere now and concentrate on naval and air power. I hope India's not politically naive about things. I won't go on here about it because I worry about the mail at this end and will look for people travelling to India to write the letters I really want to write to a few people back home like yourself. We have not seen Sujitand Kitty since they moved but spoke over the phone New Year's. My eldest son will be graduating in May from Oberlin with a philosophy degree. I don't know what he plans after that, and naturally I worry. He will go on the graduate school eventually, and will have to start paying off his loans. I wish I could send him off to India for a year or so, to you, to my aunts so he can learn a few things, perhaps under your guidance. That sort of thing ought to be happening, and perhaps one day soon it will. I wish now I had the money to do this, but it too is part of my despair.

O Sitakant. How wrong I have been. I miss India and wish that I had never come here. Except for my

husband and children and perhaps 4 or 5 friends there
has been nothing to sustain me here. I knew little of hate
and violence and racism and distrust. We are not taught in
India to hate and look down on other religions, countries,
cultures. When I left I was eager to learn, to travel and
all the world's differences were things for pleasure and
excitement, not for negative comparison making. I have
tried not to let those aspects of America's psychological
make-up become mine, but it has been hard not to be
disfigured by it. I think that if I returned to India and
stayed there for a while, I could heal myself a little we must
ally ourself securely on the side of the weak and the poor
people and nations of the world, without any compromise
with the real fascists.

What is it like now? What are you doing in Delhi?
When will you visit again? ls there anything I can send
you? How is your writing? l have written a long poem for
Kabir and I will send it to you when next someone goes.
I wonder if you could do me the favour of sending me
names and addresses of some Indian poetry journals I can
submit to. I would prefer recognition from my countrymen,
more than anything else. I have already been solicited by
Poetry Chronicle, but would like a few more names and the
address of the Illust. weekly. Is Pritish Nandy[27] still editor?
I hope not, but never mind that.

We have not seen Miki and Mary for a long time.
Occasionally we speak on the phone. 2 weeks ago I called
Miki to ask about a property in Cuttack. Peter was home
on a visit from New York City. Now he graduated from
Harvard in May and is working in Mitsubishi.

I have not heard from my uncle in Ann Arbor since
last summer on telephone. Last fall I met Shahid Agha

---

[27] Indian poet and journalist, later served in the parliament from
1998-2004, representing Shiv Sena, a Hindu nationalist party.

Ali[28] who is a splendid poet. He teaches in Ithaca[29] but has been in India on sabbatical, due to return in May I believe. Bharati Mukherji is the Indian star of the moment. She holds a significant chair at Berkeley. I wish I could get more excited about her work though but can't.

Earlier this month the Rochester region suffered an icestorm made it look like as if made of glass. It caused huge damage to practically every tree in the city, huge branches fell leaving gaping wounds, gashes. I have never seen anything like it powerlines were down everywhere and telephones. We slept in front of our wood-burning fireplace and went over to friends who still had heat, during the day and to eat. On the same block, one or two houses would have all services, but most on the same block would not. It took almost 2 weeks to restore all power and the crews are still cleaning up the branches that broke and fell under the weight of ice. The evergreens did not sustain damage, only the deciduous—all the great ancient copper beeches I love so much on the stately avenue have been struck. Schools and much else was closed for an entire week. Hendrik sorely needed that break just then because he has not been well and his children this year are the unruliest in years.

Kabir just turned 12. Tonight he has invited 4 friends to sleep over, eat pizza and to watch movies. He is wonderful and is kind to me. Kinder than I am to him. I am not a model wife and mother god knows but I do try and pray that my children will learn quickly to forgive my failings. In spite of the lifelong strain I have had with my mother, I am beginning to appreciate that she could not have found me a model daughter. I wish I could make it up

---

[28] More commonly known as Agha Shahid Ali; Shahid's name was Shahid Ali; "Agha" is an honorific that can come before or after one's name.

[29] Shahid taught at Hamilton College in Clinton, NY at the time.

to her, but being this far and poor does not help. I am full of regrets. I love India and genuinely yearn for it. The blood in me goes uphill towards it. I can understand now why in earlier times exile was punishment worse than death for certain ranks of people. Although no one has imposed exile on me, my circumstances including now my health have made it impossible for me to return or to travel anywhere.

Please forgive my errors on this machine. I never learned how to type and the keys are sticky as well. H. gave me this word processor, my very own, for my last birthday. It is a portable metallic gray/black Panasonic which I have named 'beloved'. I have not yet learned all its functions but it is a machine of enchantment you must get one for yourself. How does your garden grow? Shall I send you some seeds? Tell me what kinds. Perhaps if anyone is coming you can let me know ahead of time and they can take some back. The American poet Cornelius Eady is garnering jobs and glory like a lion. I had spoken to you of him. He heads the writing program at SUNY in Binghamton and has just come out with a new volume of poems: The Gathering of My Name (Carnegie-Mellon). It is good, but hasn't hit the bookstands as yet.

The days are still gray and often chilly. The crocus are out and I've had clumps of snowdrops (my favourite flower of the W. hemispheres which my father showed me as a child in England. I can still see clearly the crackled beige and blue pitcher with a small chip at its mouth. In which we tried unsuccessfully to force one winter).

I hunger for news of India—the political Situation—Kashmir and the communal riots. I count on you to enlighten me. Tell me what new writers and artists are about I should know of.

In these last few years I have been giving much thought to faith, including questions I would like to ask

my Hindu brothers and sisters—do they too encounter
despair, a loss of faith or doubt the way many Christians in
the West—at least the more interesting ones in our bloody
times, where the floor keeps turning do? Not too long ago
I picked up the Gita again, the translation by Isherwood
and was dazzled and moved far more intensely than the
first time in the arrogance of my youthful disbelief and
irreverence for all religions. It is a very subtle and shaded
philosophy and capable of accommodating intellectually
rigourous questioning and discrimination my own nature
seems prone to however modestly. Buddhism, which I find
anti-intellectual and aesthetically dissatisfying; too easily
lending itself to formulas (I find my relatively recently
acquired prejudices spring from my distrust and dislike of
the D. Lama) and to fascist tendencies in host cultures. Did
you know that the CIA was training Tibetans in the 50s
and early 60s in Colorado. Ahh Messrs. Ginsberg, Snyder,
Justice, Waldman etc. Sitakant, please let me know if this
letter gets through to you with unbroken seal. Of course
that is a patently silly request. Nevertheless.

What writing are you doing? How did your book sell?
Good Reviews? Do let me know. I will close now and get
this off today. It has been sitting too long in 'beloved'. My
best regards to Basanti. Send me photographs. Are you a
grandfather yet?

sincerely, affectionately,
Shreela.

209 Dartmouth Street
Rochester. New York
14607
9 April, 1991

Mr. Peter McWalters, Superintendent
131 West Broad Street
Rochester City School District
Rochester, N.Y, 14614

Dear Mr. McWalters,

In mid-March my husband and l received a letter from Ms.
Marcia Reichardt notifying us that our sixth grader Kabir
(#58) had not been admitted to Wilson Jr. High. We had
accepted the decision, and our son will learn to live with
this disappointment. I called the office merely to inquire
about his status on the waiting list, and what, if anything,
could be done fairly and reasonably to hope. The young
woman who took my call said she would send me an appeal
form. I have not yet received it.

When Ms. Reichardt called me later that day I
wanted to know what some of the criteria for admission
were. Her reaction aroused more curiosity and questions
than my original intentions for calling deserved. I inquired
whether East Indian was a minority category (along with
gender and siblinghood) in the search for racial/ethnic
variety and balance. She connected me with Ms. Ann
Pennella from whom I learned that requests for ethnic
minority statistics—like much else—must be in writing.
Such facts and figures are not confidential but can be made
available to a curious and civic member of the community
through your desk. There is some confusion over what the
minority in question is called. Here I gathered that there
are four options and I will name them all to avoid delays

in communication: East Indian, Oriental; Asian and Other. I trust that if the right person at the right computer will ask the right question and push the right button, to get the correct answer will not take too much time. I will close by stating the two questions I would gratefully like answered:

(1) What is Kabir de Leeuw's standing on the waiting list and by what criteria are selections from this list made?
(2) How many (%) students of East-Indian (one or both parents) attend Rochester City Schools?

Thank you for your time. I look forward to hearing from you.

Sincerely,
Shreela Ray.

11/4/91

Dearest Gawain,

In front of me are 10 daffodils from our yard Hendrik picked Sunday. They are standing strong and bold announcing themselves in the blue Chinese vase I like so much. I say announcing because I am reading Bruce Chatwin's (Songlines, do you know it?) about how Australia's aborigines believe man created the universe by singing everything into existence. I like the idea. But it is not just another anthro-travel book. He has so many other little things tucked away in his storytelling to delight and recommend, that I have been mentioning it to everyone. It is a thin book and quite readable. Here is a passage I marked that appealed to me and which I pass on to you:

The definition of a man's 'own country'—as 'the place in which I do not have to ask' yet to feel 'at home' in that country depended on being able to leave it.

That is the essence, but it is followed by:

'Everyone hoped to have at least four 'ways out', along which he could travel in a crisis. Every tribe—like it or not—had to cultivate relations with its neighbor.

That is sort of where I suppose you are at present, in a manner of speaking. You should have as many choices. You seem to have far more than I did, even. Though I was years out of the country at your age when I graduated with no useful skill. You have more financial opportunities (I was not allowed to work more than 20 hrs pw or off-campus) and a family, ways of acquiring marketable skills to make travel and job types more various, language, typing, auto mechanics, household repair, etc. You do have some computer literacy and your bartending license. I'm not yet convinced of the US or worldwide marketability of this, or how a prospective employer will react if it looks that given time for self improvement and skill acquisition, that is what you chose.

I will stop in a moment. This will be my last such letter to you. Our work is finished but I would like to say these things to you. You are young and healthy. I hope you don't go only for the safe and sure job, thing, place or person. I wish I could see you stick to some one thing outside your 'academic' life that you followed through and mastered, and worked to save for travel somewhere. It is not too late to acquire a practical skill and be better grounded in a language. There are immersion courses offered in various places during the summer; in NY state through the SUNY system, there was one at New Paltz I think. I know Oberlin has been good for you but you can't stay there forever, expecting people to keep your self-confidence up. That can and must finally only come from within yourself if it is to mean something at all at the end. I wish now that people had not indulged me and told me I had talent. Obviously I don't, and certainly not enough to have warranted the time, effort and money (other people's) I wasted on it. I should have spent it on something less reliant on such subjective criteria. You are genuinely intelligent and smarter and there is no reason why you should make the same mistakes I made. Now looking back, I see my life a gigantic hoax in which I am the main victim and perpetrator. You can imagine what that does to my self esteem and hope in life. Library science, medicine, marine biology, even secretary would have been better. Don't sell yourself short by limiting yourself to opportunities by relying so heavily on other people's good words to make you feel good. It is nice, but not enough. You are bright and able, so go for it and get out of there. What are you afraid of? You have both my respect and love. Everyone I know talks about you AS IF YOU ARE SOME KIND OF SAINT AND super-counselor. I worry that you give too much time to other people and do not spend enough of it on yourself, thinking, listening, reading more 'literature' than I suspect you do, but I know in college, unless you are in lit. courses it is difficult to do so. You must learn to be by yourself more qualitatively because once you get a job in earnest you will not have as much time as you think you will.

I often feel that you misread much of what I have said or believed in. When I urge care in dress and table manners, knives and forks it is not because they are ends in themselves but because they are ways of giving you some sort of power to go anywhere in the world and know what to do, they help make you unobtrusive so you can pay attention more to persons and more important things around you (learn to eat with your hand and chopsticks as well), and importantly, to help make the world more beautiful, at least, remember that people are looking at you too- and dress clean and carefully does not mean to be pre-occupied with dress but that balance that gives others' eyes pleasure and rest without drawing due attention,—or dress so modestly, so that you blend in with the environment. Modesty may be good there. You can reserve your pride and display on other things of greater substance. Anyway. Enough of that too. I love you very much Gawain. I don't mean to live my life over in you, but I will pass on my own experiences as a perspective and a mother's right to do so and you are perfectly within your rights to choose what you wish from it or not at all. Usually, you will do what you think best for yourself. I will confess to one anxiety, and that is if you were to choose to fight in a war and a US one specially.

Arthur Schram (do you remember Pieter & Ineke of Rutgers who used to take care of you at 18 mos. or so?

217

They were very close friends. He, a physicist at UR. Art
is their son) a bigwig economist is going to be at Harvard
for the summer and lecturing in various places in the US,
will be visiting April 18, and then again often when his
parents and his wife and children arrive over the summer.
I do hope you will meet them. It must be a priority. Also,
our 25 wedding anniversary will be with the Buhler's in
Princeton at the fabulous, new house they plan to buy,
and we intend to make it a big affair. Of course we will
have little to say about the kind of extravaganza, but it
will be fun nevertheless. I think it is important to send
grad. invitations to Care, Shirrell and Rollo, Tom and
Jeanne, Peter Keenan (he and Mackenzie have separated.
Sad), Jim and Julie. Others possibly, McCoys, Ingrid,
Garlock. Maybe a short note to Ms. Chapman c/o #58
and to Ms. Signer. Also my mother and Bugul, and the
Ranihat Ray family are important. It will make them
happy to get any word from you.

Charles is making the most beautiful quilt for
himself. It is a spectacular piece of stitching and design
although quite simple to look.

I made it to Easter Sunday Service. Did you? I also
have been trying desperately to get on with the writing. I
want to do a series of religious poems on Bible passages that
I remember from my childhood that return to me now, and
have been reading Act and Letters of St. Paul over again and
quite enjoying them, if such one can say. But people keep
distracting me. Cate has sailed in, Corny and Sara. Corny's
father is very ill in the hospital. Oh yes, Send them an
invitation or announcement too. I will enclose the addresses.

Michael Swain will be here for his degree when we
are at Oberlin. I also sent a card off to Elizabeth. Don't
forget Babu either. Again, please remember these are
finally up to you. Dustbooks sent me $41 in royalties. I

will enjoy the idea for a few more days and then send it back. It took almost two years of letters and phone calls to get him to respond to although it was not the royalties I wanted from him.

Gawain, you must not get yourself into situations where other people get you out of financial crunches or buy you things (the $200 clothing situation Sears you found yourself recently and Jerome and eye glasses etc. etc.) It seems a little demeaning, doesn't it? As Polonius said to his son Laertes, in a very good speech I might add in spite of the fact that P. is held to ridicule in much received critical lits. "Neither a borrower nor a lender be . . ." check it out.

I'm wondering what to give you for graduating. Any ideas? I hope we will see a lot of you.

Kabir did not get into Performing Arts magnet and is a little disappointed. Hendrik's back is acting up a bit. My breathing is not doing so well at the present but it will. I am impatient to get into the yard. We have had 2-3 glorious days, but unreliable. Suddenly it will get chilly and gray. Great thunder showers, lightning and winds. On Sunday we cooked out with Verhults. First of the season.

How is the paper coming? I'm sure it will be fine. I don't accept your excuse about audience. The problems I saw would still be the same, but by no means absolute or un-correctable. You have enough time. It seems to me that the real problem is that you have read too much and not allowed for enough cogitation, for the material to settle and sink in this could be out of anxiety and panic. relax. Remember you have the skills, at least, when I think of your WM paper of years ago, I know you could do it did. Don't forget, I want a final copy for my scrap book.

Write. Or call late. Love from us both and Kabir. God bless.

your mother.

26/11/91

My dear Bill and Jean,

This may or may not be the letter I have been meaning to
write since about 5 years ago in response to a remark of
Bill's: 'we respond to what we recognize' (approx.), the exact
context of which I forget at the moment, but if I were to try
doing that now, this letter will take another 5 years and be
ten times as long which will be misery for us all.

I dug up my Mentor paperback Gita transl. by
Isherwood and his Swami Prabhavananda, intro. by
Huxley, (pub. in'42), still available and I have a copy for
you. Mine is too marked up with my 'Christian' Pauline
and Augustinian responses, i.e. all that talk of Maya,
illusion. figures of 'seeing', the eye, veils between the
corporeal world and Spirit -spirit and flesh, body and
soul. Here let me state very generally that in the US
Hinduism has been less attractive than Buddhism. This
has not always been the case. Remember Emerson and the
Brahmins—but more on them wait. I think there is a level
at which Buddhism is more materialistic, i.e. serves mental
and Other body faculties 'needs' which has resulted in an
interest in 'mental' constructions or a healthy life, mind
and body, this worldliness (health foods and body building),
and would account for Buddhism's success through Zen
and Chinese forms in complex society cultures with strong
organized martial traditions; not for defending any pie in
the sky. Its systems can tolerate, better yet, beautify common
garden varieties of atheism and dull agnosticism, but for
those who have ever known or been bitten by the God bug,
even once, the ideas of the human soul as immortal and/
or Divine spirit, the Omnipotent and benevolent etc. the
Gita's distinction of 'Spirit' as realities, truths to be sought.

Buddhism offers non-beingness; nothing. In the 20th cent. after two wars the Judeo-Protestant darkness can more readily accept this (I see the courtship of the Dalai Lama recent years as part of the New World Order), I can't. It is unscientific. At least the other two (three actually—Islam and Judaism & pre-war Christianity) offer something one can call altered states. But now I'm getting into other things I don't mean to at present. Hang in there. At the end of chpt. III, Karma Yoga:

'The senses are said to be higher than the sense-objects. The mind is higher than the senses. The intelligent will is higher than (and here we begin the leap) the mind. What is higher than the intelligent will? The Atman Itself.'

Check out 1 Corinth. chpt.13, 14:15 : 'I will sing with the spirit, and I will sing with the mind.' Also. Not to mention Paul's constant harping on the body/soul , spirit/flesh thing which I think he meant quite differently (closer to Vedic?) than the Church made him to represent.

But let me finish off the Gita passage above because knowing you, you will make much merry with it (ho ho ho; we have our Hindu puritans too): '. . . Get control of the mind through spiritual discrimination then destroy your elusive enemy, who wears the form of lust.' p. 49 (Ho ho ho; we have our Hindu puritans too.)

Also check out Romans v.20 –

'Ever since the creation of the world, his invisible nature . . . has been clearly perceived in the things that have been made.' chpt. 12 v 4 'For as in one body we have many members and all the members do not have the same function, so we, though many, are one in body in Christ, and individually members one of another. Having gifts which differ according to the grace given us, let us use them: if prophecy, in proportion to our faith; if service, in our serving; . . .' etc.

Also Rom. 14, could be written in defense of caste
system tolerance? As I ended up reading all the letters of
Paul I concluded that 'perhaps' I had got things the wrong
way around. How Eastern is his thought, but why not?
There was probably greater movements, exchanges beyond
commercial trade than we realize and are willing to admit
(?). But regardless of which way things went or came, this
is heady stuff. (And what a pity not many people read it
any more. On the other hand I suppose there is a way of
reading it too, and the age era/epoch that made it possible
for me is gone forever, and I am sad. Should I not be? Shall
I hope and say it will be better read, enjoyed, interpreted?) I
gave up. Time for a break. Marking too many passages.

"Freedom from activity is never achieved from
abstaining from action. Nobody can become perfect
by simply ceasing to act . . . The truly admirable man
controls his senses by his power of his will . . . The world
is imprisoned in its own activity, except when actions are
performed as worship of God. Therefore you perform every
action sacramentally, and be free from all attachments to
results." KARMA YOGA III

(Pure Act)

'You cannot see me with those human eyes.
Therefore I give you divine sight' (Gita) Also Paul to
Romans: the Spirit himself intercedes for us with sighs too
deep for words (8,v.26). Paul blinded enroute to Damascus?

Nearby he also mentions the groaning' Spirit (I sort
of like that too) . . .

Anyway, the point is, there is way too much. Best
would be if you read Rom, both Corinthians, Galatians
and Hebrews. Galatians because it says something about
'faith coming as revelation (3 v.15) AND thereby HAS

EGALITARIAN EFFECTS among others. But read the Gita. Concurrently. You'll see what I mean. They share the exhortatory quality too, naturally I was struck by the personal tenderness Krishna shows Arjuna because I had been misled into not expecting it, forgetting the great Bhakti traditions of [Krishna] and Mirabai. Hannah Arendt, somewhere, I read makes much of Paul's 'personal god' as a distinctive feature of Christianity. I also found myself wondering about Atman as the ultimate object of contemplation.

But there is also this breathing, the breath of God, the sacred syllable Om, the Word, the yoga practices, to breathe also arid to receive it and exhale it. Bill, on the phone you mentioned Olson which reminds me now of hearing him speak of 'the word' and 'breath' in some connection archetypal at that one class called Myth and Lit.

Paul also speaks of 'faith in his heart' and of not making 'mental reservations' 'by his grace you will find peace' It seems to me in the Gita, the purpose of life is to know (contemplate forever) the supreme Reality, and I underline know rather than Reality—they are the one and the same anyway. Is it the Beatific Vision of Aquinas? I think this is worthy of thought. But also some funny things happened. e.g.in BG. [Gita] chpt. XIII is The Field and the Knower. As I understood it I thought this truly was a concept I had not come across anywhere else or quite so expressed, that I am the body observing itself, or am what observes & divine too. I was quite thrilled by it and the poetic possibilities it opened up. Then I remembered Yeats. This is probably where he too stumbled for Michael Robartes. Anyway, it seemed to me, (I misunderstood it) the Field, even without hypothesis of God, gave me a vehicle for human relationships; the severity with which one experiences apartness; like I and Thou; that I know and take my being against yours, the other, and vice versa,

even if we can't meet to cross, falling in space in parallel
lines (Calvinolike). But I also felt sad coming across one
of those places where what I could agree with or accept
intellectually, I may want to renounce. If I were Arjuna to
ask, profoundly stupid, can there be a Hindu existentialist
(my god out of all this chaos in my head a poem must be
born. Prose simply will not do). If love of friends, husband,
child is illusion then I choose illusion; I say, but I like it
here. It's not always this bad, and even if it is, it's my bad.
So I am condemned forever like Sisyphus? It would be
dishonest for me to say there are days when I find myself
thinking of a plain old Christian heaven 'where those angel
faces smile' or the 'road I walked with my sweet Mary' sort
of thing, or at best Pilgrim at the Celestial city. But then I
am ashamed and embarrassed. Most of the time everything's
quietly tormenting. True Catholic, hope filled Christianity
and Hinduism offer acceptable ends. Why do I resist? No.
it's not that I resist but . . .

Hebrews 11, v. 1 'The world was created by the word
of God, so that what is seen was made out of things which
do not appear.'

And you must read Cor. 2 Cornth 2, v 14: fragrance of
the knowledge of him everywhere . . . to one a fragrance from
death to death, to the other a fragrance from life to life . . .

As a young girl and woman I went through all the
usual postures and stages and fashions of disbelief, and I
don't apologize for that but I also think that much of the
time (until Gawain was about to begin middle-school) I
allowed myself to be embarrassed intimidated into a kind
of self-exile from the Spirit by those for whom religion was
exotic or repressive. And faith [is] a murky thing. There are
many who do not distinguish faith from the materialistic
forms of official religion. Catholics I know are particularly
expressive of anger and bitterness. Now I say I'm sorry they

dislike their religion but it does not seem right to castigate or penalize me or mine. A category I specially disliked were those who were disappointed in my not being a Hindu or Buddhist or Jain. Many were actually vicious. I remember once in the early '70s a philosopher atheist angrily demanded why I cared about what happened in Vietnam or anywhere else for that matter and I was so startled that anyone could ask another human that question, I couldn't say anything for a while and when I did, it was a cop-out political response entirely in keeping with the marketplace. What I really wanted to say was 'you mean you don't?' and 'because I am a Christian and my brother's keeper,' but I am not so cowardly now. Also the Gita makes a big point of saying that the action is more important than the outcome. It is unswerving and simple and beautiful in that insistence.

Dec. 9 :

Weeks have gone by. I will end this soon. After writing the above pages, Charles brought down his two translations. One is a very scholarly and dense one by a Dutchman J. Ao Bo Buitenen, and I am told, the most excellent. There is another good one by Barbara Stoler-Miller in quatrains. Isherwood's is the most eccentric but I think Stoller-Miller comes close to him for demonstrating my St. Paul point. If I were to recommend a version for someone on the run, I would suggest Isherwood first. If they get turned·, they will know how to pursue it. [Barbara Stoler-Miller] a close second. In her book: I learned that Gandhi himself came to read the Gita after Thoreau who had been introduced to it by Emerson. In Walden Thoreau writes about seeing slabs of ice being cut by East Ind. Co. men to ship to India. Imagine. And makes much more of this in another work I don't know, but have something about a Week on the Merrimac (?). He

is interested in the Hindu concept of action and human
perfection in the light of human imaginative creativity; Yes
Life to life, fragrance to fragrance, ideas. Gandhi took much
on—civil disobedience from Thoreau who in turn got it Gita
etc. etc., not to forget Martin LK.

       Re. CIA and Rajiv.[30] Yes but not in the usual way.
I think what has happened is that the CIA has successfully
established native operatives everywhere (one doesn't need
too many) in all walks and classes, intellectual, business,
media, labour etc. and in India, castes too. And has trained
them and provided them with materials etc. But these will
function autonomously, sometimes even against each other
. . . Kurds, Afghanis and would be hard to control. The US
(perhaps the West) does not want a Non-aligned superpower.
In India the Nehru/Gandhi name is the last one left. (In
the whole world?) of world political leaders coming out
from WWII Anglo/European cultural and political tastes.
This includes families (I still fancy myself a welfare state
socialist) like mine. Those of us who could move and
pass in 'cultured' European circles and had Western style
(meaning English) educations. I remember saying foolishly,
to my mother during a quarrel when she first came in '69
when Gawain was born that India would never be free
until we had buried her and my father's generation. Of
course I was speaking figuratively, and of course it was a
terrible thing to say, and of course I was misunderstood
and I shouldn't have said it, and of course I was right, the
difference is, I now wish it wasn't. The CIA is successful

---

[30] Rajiv Gandhi, the son of Indira Gandhi and grandson of
Jawaharlal Nehru, was elected prime minister of India upon the
assassination of his mother in 1984 and served in that office until
1989. He was assassinated in May of 1991 by a member of the Tamil
Tigers, a Tamil separatist organization based in Sri Lanka. Here
(and below) Shreela seems to entertain a different theory as to Rajiv
Gandhi's assassination.

because there are enough Indians (out of 800 million more than anywhere else) who are corrupt and corruptible, or million more than anywhere else) who are corrupt and corruptible, or are naïve and cannot see the large picture. Once in a while we get a renegade, Amin, Noriega. But anyway, whenever I go back I am amazed to see and hear the intensity with which people hate an entire family for several generations (some might mutter something about Nehru or his sister being different) without any personal contact with them at all.

My brother and I elicit weird responses. Specially me. There is also another significant factor at work. The US is now the place for higher education. Until the mid-60s England and Germany. Then things changed quite dramatically. Those who first went to England came from Upper class/castes. Now we have the entrepreneurial castes/classes coming to the US (I myself was expected to go to England but said Nay vigorously) this is a form of 'democratization' of course, and that is a good thing, but somewhere in there is some doubts, distrust, after my last visit and when I meet some of my countrymen here.

I'm convinced all the Gandhi children will be killed.

I liked Indira G. I think she had ideals but was also a pragmatist and understood how important the principles of compromise,—including manipulation-were in a multi-cultural country like India, and she was determined to keep India unified.

I don't think it was the Tamils. Under the 'disguise' of secessionist groups, it could have been the CIA -do you know that when she was voted back into power after Janata fell in the late 70's, early 8O's, the Ford foundation sponsored a conference right under her nose in Delhi, in which members of the Indian Intelligentsia and professional groups, discussed ways and means of preventing her from returning to power in the future? Still, I am not too satisfied this time that they were as directly involved and encouraging as they were with Mrs. Gandhi's [assassination].

And now I believe that as long as Israelis are mercenaries to train Indian army or otherwise in Kashmir, India loses all claims to it. Does the world really need another region in which Jews and Muslims will hate each other. That Hindu India should hire Jews to keep a Muslim state is too much.

Well I will stop for now. I've taken way too much of your time, but you were not meant to read this all at once. I have started trying to put a book together and the work is going slowly. I have a lot, but I throw a lot away easily.

Being very forgetful, I don't know where you will be for Christmas. I hope all is well. I've been reading all kinds of wonderful things, some of them re-reading, a little Apollinaire (in trans. of course), and Phyllis Thompson stopped by briefly on her way to Yaddo and it was good to see her in high spirits, decked with wonderful large rings on her fingers, and fine necklaces of the S. West around her neck. She has new poems and we were able to talk and gossip a bit.

Gawain is home working at a day-care centre and has started applying to grad schools already.

I hope we see you soon. Take care, Merry Christmas and happy New Year too, from us all.

love,

c: Ann Pennella
Marcia Reichardt

29/11/91

My dear Munna Bhai,

Just recently I learnt about Shanti Mausi's death. There is nothing one can say of course, but I grieve too, even now because she was so much a part of my joyful & innocent past.

I owe Anna Liese a letter from quite some time back. Dine also says that she broke a leg. How is that doing? When did this happen? Lalit has not been in touch with us for years although we keep getting mail for him over here. I have no idea as to where we should send it so we send it back. Are you grandparents yet? What are you all doing with yourselves? Please write and tell me. Also, can't you come to the States on a visit? I would love to see you. In another 4 years Hendrik could retire and we thought of returning to India to at least try, but I have health problems that make it nigh impossible. You don't know how much I ache for India. I should never have come to this country and were it not for Hendrik and my children and a few friends there is nothing for me, specially in terms of work, which of course is imperative to anyone's life.

By the way, I have discovered the Gita. I had no idea it was such a fabulous thing. I began reading it together with the letters of St. Paul and that is quite a revelatory thrill. I am convinced there must have been great intercourse between those regions of the world because so many of the concepts, seem similar; illusion, matter and body, that will is an active force, the belief in the after life although here there may be a real difference though, but still, I have been quite excited and comforted by it. I did not know that Gandhi had not read it seriously until much later in his life, and even then was turned onto it by way of that wonderful American Thoreau who read it in the first half of the 19 century and was taken by it too. Do you know that ice was being shipped to India from America in 1845?

We are ok. Gawain graduated in May and is now working to save money for grad school and to begin paying off some of his college loans. He likes philosophy and he is heading for divinity school. We don't know where that will be. I wish he would go to India on a trip he saves up for, but I think he is a little afraid of it because the pain he has seen in me and misunderstood. I will send him to both of you for sure, so he can meet a few of the best and dearest I left but have always yearned for you will show him how wonderful India is too; the little things; never mind the big ones the big problems everyone complains about but the ordinary, everyday quiet things that I felt still existed in Orissa and perhaps all over rural India. How long this will be, God knows. The barbarians are everywhere, the dogs of greed. Was it always this way and only the forms are different?

Have you built a house yet? If so, describe it to me, or what you plan to build. Make sure you have a little room for Hendrik and me when we visit and enough space for me to put a typewriter on. Maybe if you have a large piece of land we can buy a little piece on it in one corner for a little house for ourselves. Hendrik and I will take charge of the garden, vegetable, herb and flower. Hendrik knows how to make beer, what more does one need except a handful of people one loves and I my books and writing. Hendrik plays the guitar and recorder. Perhaps you can take up something, how about the violin or sitar or tabla?

Well I'm coming to the end of this and hope it comes out ok on the WordP. If I get chopped off, don't worry I'll write it in by hand somewhere if it is important. My love to you all. Please drop me a line, it would make me very happy.

But again, my heart is with you, and heavy

love,

3/3/92

My dear Shahid,

It was good to have you here even though you slaved to produce a splendid meal for my friends and family, and didn't have much time to relax and do your own things. This is meant to be a longer, ruminative letter, but I just blew the monitor on my Olivetti and am having a bad time with my back-up Panasonic , so can't see what I am writing to you, and so have to keep it short. Perhaps for your sake, that is good.

I gave your book to the Summers and am enclosing payment for it and your translations.[31] Thank you very much for both of them. Enclosed is my payment. I feel strongly that friends must pay for poetry books, specially by one's friends, otherwise who will these days?

I hope I'll see you once again before you go. You are a good person Shahid. I feel sisterly and hope you do not think me forward for saying so. I didn't realize how cynical I must have become. Do you think there is any cure for it?

I'm going to send this off to you today, and pray that they can fix my Olivetti quickly so that I can write the letter and poems I have to, for you. Take care, and thanks a million again.

cheers,
Shreela

---

[31] *The Rebel Silhouette*, Agha Shahid Ali's translations of Faiz Ahmed Faiz had just been released.

13/12/93

My dear Bill,

I like your 'chthonian' voice idea because of something I
had read not too long ago about 'memory'. Can there be
something like the 'collective unconscious', a thread . . .
An English scientist, (his name escapes me at the moment)
widely respected speaks of 'memory' as not located centrally
but all over the brain, revealing at various times, deep
memories.

I recant the nonsense about multi-cultural stuff. I
think I was trying to console both of us. The fact is, I am a
little envious and resentful specially since self-righteously I
think I have been 'professionally' chaste and high-minded.
The new students coming from the sub-continent at least
are far more familiar with the new social sciences, their
native histories and languages & in many instances have
the new tech/computer skills.

If I understand you correctly, I agree with you when
you say 'the populist rhetoric of the time led to highly
elitist theorizing . . . and the triumph of theorizing from
which the humanities never recovered.' I am a product
of the same Anglo/European centered education as you
are. These 'new' folk who are displacing us faster than we
can adjust, and who after all have come to stay, and are
'globally' educated. I don't know if this means better or not.
I was wrong to speak so ignorantly, specially since I am in
many ways sympathetic 'politically and socially' to them,
but perhaps not intellectually.

The multiculturalists demand at least equal time with
the old canons, and/or opportunity to help devise a new one
and a new set of theory/theories to go with it. European in
its origins (and then to find de Man grandfather of them all
already here), in one form transported by Third Worlders

and a Sephardic Jew and received by others already here.
What is interesting to me is that an outstanding % of these
'multi' people are themselves 'colonized Americans,' i.e.
Blacks, women, Hispanics, Nat. American. etc. etc . . . I find
it interesting that the poetry/intellectuals sent abroad to sell
the American way are those who best make a case for rugged
romantic individualism (a la Whitman): Ginsberg, Kinnell
for the young faddist pinkos of a new India (Commonwealth
countries). Someone said to me vis-à-vis England's immigrant
situation, the chickens have come home to roost. Yes but
also by having Ginsberg & Co. peddling Walt/Williams
for Uncle Sam the US has taken up the role that Engl.,
Europe and the BIBLE (O & NT) had in making you and
me. The enemies of "India" came from the Western break
in the Khyber pass and from the Western side of the Ind.
Ocean on ships. Good Hindus were not allowed to cross
those black waters although in the case of Gandhi and
Ramanujan exceptions divine clearance was given. There are
no postscripts to airships, airwaves, telecommunications etc.,
radio free Europe, voice of America and the Trojan Horse
of heady free market systems. Religion bound India e.g.
freedom were sent abroad poked around in them I was quite
alarmed. Such thinking can bring us into the lotus position
of fascism. And how do we talk ourselves out of that one?
What I meant to have said was there are disturbing aspects
to this. I think people like Mukherji and others with some
modest talents or skills have then brought over part of pax
americana intellectuals via Iowa City/Brockport, other spots
all over the country. It is US gov. paranoia and ambition for
the hearts and minds of everybody that is the driving force
behind much of this multi-cult stuff & the hostility to it.
Imperial England is dead, even as intellectual centre of the
commonwealth, and the US has replaced her. I mean look at
Rushdie, logically he belongs to England as I do, but by freak

he shows up on these shores where we are to assume he will
be safest. The problem is I am sympathetic that 'other' voices
be heard, and that people make new things from old, for that
is how things go on. Shakes. and Chaucer will never die,
even with a 25 year moratorium. The new writers seem very
clever, smarter than I am about many things, still, I think
my education is more accommodating and more rigorous,
and whenever I can, in my few forays into fiction I enjoy
applying the aesthetic principles of 'my' tradition. The truth
is the people best in position to separate chaff from dress are
the few like yourself. Our 'classics' will always be read by the
true lovers of lit. But that still leaves room for new work, and
I know you have been so open to things different, new, that
what the multi-cult need is some of the best of the 'old' guard
to clear their heads and to bring their training, minds and
gifts to the new work. (I loved my education but it was an
elitist's one; lots of dead wood, rubbish, and double standards
that seriously needed re-hauling. (Years ago in the course of
a quarrel I said to my mother, 'India will never be free until
you and your generation is dead and buried'). People I do
respect who know these things agree that Morrison indeed. I
read The Color Purple and I hated it.

I think novels have always been a 'commodity',
linked with the ring of mercantilism so it would be absurd
for me to claim otherwise.

For a relatively brief moment in the 20th century
an attempt to exalt fiction as a 'high' literary genre-,
concurrent, most certainly ipso facto, was made. The audio-
visual technology world-wide appears to have necessitated
quick-turnovers, so no one is literary king/queen for much
longer than a week or two.

I think you had the key when you said you didn't
think this 'multi-cultural' thing would last very long.

*These are two brief notes Shreela wrote while in the hospital at the
end of her life.*

They were written around August 12 or 13, 1994.

My country, my sister,
Only the poor do forever what the gods should
They sit in the hard white sun motionless
Swatting the fly, gnat
Turning the creaking fan, forever

A day later:

Worst hospitalization at Genesee.
Le Pen is an oriental ogress, petite,
femme fatale wrote one hard, dense skeletal poem,
hands shaking from spray atrovent.
My wonderful friends Ingrid,
today Ruth and Carter yesternight
great crossings for me over the dark desert.

ESSAYS

"IN THE NIGHTS OF THIS RUNAWAY EXILE": ON SHREELA RAY'S POETICS OF FIRST PLACE AND (NON)ARRIVAL

Rohan Chhetri

Reading Shreela Ray's poems sometimes feels to me like entering a covenant, a sense of being in the middle of an interior and exclusive conversation. An affiliation to a system of meaning, voice, syntax and emotional framework through some illusion of shared temperament. This is perhaps what Patti Smith calls "lineage" in a truer sense, a notion more private than "tradition." Where does it come from? Is it her bright and jagged voice that always seems to be speaking in the present? Is it the condition of "self-exile" that always carries a little baggage of shame that speaks to my own, issuing a forewarning in the booze-wrecked croak of Berryman in her poem "Kafka 2": "Go home go home / before this country destroys you"(lines 18-19). What is it about Ray's letters that seem like dead missives from the terminal decades of the 20th century revealing incipient cultural fault lines that are all too apparent now? Or is it simply the experience of a brown

writer trying to make a living in a predominantly white male
landscape of the burgeoning MFA industrial complex of the
70s and 80s, many of whom were her mentors & teachers like
Robert Frost, John Berryman, William Meredith?

It is no accident that Ray's work has been discovered in
the present historical moment in America, a time of revision
and reckoning, largely due to the tireless efforts of Kazim Ali;
that it is being given a long overdue life of print in a poetic
landscape that has begun finally to self-consciously center
marginalized voices, thus inverting the map significantly for
once. It is pertinent to mention here that the roadmap to
her discovery was laid out by Shreela Ray herself, through
her dogged commitment to her art and her uncompromising
stance on the local and global politics of her time, often to
the detriment of her advancement as a "career poet," and in a
poetry world that systemically and blatantly worked to make
people who looked like her "unheard of."

I also suspect the kinship I feel towards her work is one
of "lineage" in a geographical sense, something that taints,
informs and enlarges my reading of her work. Almost 60 years
before me, Ray came to America to pursue undergraduate
studies at Webster College, Missouri at the age of 18, after
completing her schooling from Loreto Convent, Darjeeling, a
hill station in the foothills of the Himalayas, once a summer
resort for the British elite. She later went on to attend the Iowa
Writers' Workshop. My own trajectory begins from a Catholic
boarding school run by Swiss missionaries in Kalimpong, a
sister city about 30 miles from Darjeeling. After a brief stint
in the publishing industry in India, I too came to America
to join a writing program, although in my late twenties.
What I'm trying to get at here, perhaps, is a recognition of
an inner geographical landscape one sees first in childhood
that lends a particular palimpsestic shade against which all
other landscapes are experienced in adulthood: "A place of

first permission / everlasting omen of what is" (Duncan 22-23). This geographical dichotomy is sharp in Ray's earliest letters. The pastoral continues to remain a potent strain in her future body of work with descriptions of landscape often acting as an "objective correlative" that evoke themes of exile, and political and cultural despair. The barren winter Mid Atlantic landscape, particularly in her later poems, becomes a field of triangulation between the exiled self and the diffusing memory of home as she struggles to "make a garden out of this place" ("Night in April," line 18).

In an early letter from 1962 written to her brother in Darjeeling, Shreela reports the New England landscape of the Breadloaf School of English where she is writing from: "The college itself is very exclusively situated on this mountain, not really a mountain compared to the Himalayas, but truly lovely." A little later in the same letter she writes about Darjeeling wistfully, "God what a country that was," designating the scale of the small Himalayan hill station to an entire "country." In the two poems we've chosen to bookend the selection in this volume, this "first" landscape emerges under an often joyful but strict shadow of the Catholic school education system. From which also emerges a certain darker strain of the legacy of colonialism, as in the poems of Eunice de Souza, whose debut collection, *Fix*, published a year later than Shreela's own Indian debut in 1979, is often considered a breakthrough in women's anglophone poetry in India. This is evident in the scenes of the forbidden girlhood chatter under the redolent Magnolia Campbellii (a deciduous tree endemic to the Himalayan valleys) hiding away from the eyes of the "good nuns" in "Five Virgins and the Magnolia Tree," a poem starkly reminiscent of Souza's "Sweet Sixteen"; or in being taught to sing Robert Herrick poems set to music by an Irish nun in the late poem, "I Sing Because I Love to Sing":

So began each singing lesson, near
the highest mountains of the world—
where I first learned to sing—
and innocently sing, ribald Herrick
on Schubert's catchy tunes . . .   (1-5)

As is often the case in Ray's work, this poem which
begins with the memory of "singing," seen as a precursor to
her poetic vocation, magnifies the condition of exile, made
more poignant by despair over her failing health which made
it increasingly impossible for her to return to India toward
the end of her life. She looks back fondly to the memory of
that freedom that her cloistered girlhood in a convent school
nonetheless afforded her:

" . . . And I ask
              as the last doors
of this land close on me
How will I restore my blindness?
How my sweet bird's broken wing?

I have enough breath to turn the page.
Who will sing alto in my place?"   (72-78)

The exile is compounded as the speaker begins to hint at
something that symbolically bars her from that freedom in
the present: a racist incident at a Church that seems to have
cemented her estrangement and her sense of non-belonging
in America. This incident is depicted in the poem "The Way
We Are":

Somewhere in Arkansas on a Sunday morning
the good people prepare for Church

. . .

Baptist USA here I come!
Enter Charlene:
"The family would prefer you don't come
To Church. Please understand the way
things are in small towns."   (1-2, 14-18)

The poem nonetheless manages to, in signature Ray fashion, bring a considered levity and a wit burnished by the otherwise enraging incident. Not once does the poem adopt the rhetoric of a victim, instead arriving toward an alternate mode of redemption through the natural world: " . . . I groped / descending in the universal ichor, / with both feet on the ground." (29-31)

The condition of self-exile in Ray's poems is characterized by a double consciousness, a transit-state of being caught in a static fugue of "arrival" and "return." We see through the arc of Ray's small body of work how this condition devolves from the novelty of immigrant experience (still present in her first letters home) to the condition of exilic despair, as if her entire life and work were spent in one long preparation for return. A return that became more impossible with each passing decade, for neither the exiled "self" nor the idea of "home" remains constant but forever caught in a state of deferral and flux. The drama of this vacillation between (non)arrival and (non)return recurs again and again in Ray's poems. For example, in "Falling Asleep" she writes:

There is no place on earth I can
undo these years . . .

The closest sea is 300 miles away.
I wish I could go home, but now
changes frighten me and the language
is not one I write in anymore . . .

. . .

It is daybreak and only now
have I brought myself to this place.   (21-24, 30-31)

As evident in the final two lines of the poem, the points
of arrival are multiple and hence non-existent, or rather they
are a series of "rehearsals" of arrival. The poem is haunted
by the famous twin last lines in modern poetry: Rilke's "You
must change your life" (line 14) and James Wright's "I have
wasted my life" (line 13). Echoing Wright in the same poem
("A chicken hawk floats over, looking for home."[12]), Ray
looks for emblems of the divided self in the natural world in
"Snow Buddha":

After all these years I learn
that the brown sparrow cooped
in dazzling America complains
of the winter . . .   (10-13)

In Ray's case, sometimes this "complaint" morphs into
elaborate fantasies of "unreturning" as in the poems written
during one of her infrequent visits to India. In the "Road to
Puri" she writes, " . . . I don't want to go back to America /
or to change the fabric / of my first body" (19-21). However,
this particular fantasy of "unreturning" and the reinstatement
back from exile ("I want to sleep with a man / raised on dahl
and rice" (23-24)) is quickly dismantled as she sees a little
further ahead on the road "a man digging / a small trench by
his house" (26-27). The figure reminds her of her suburban
life in the US and her American husband, "my yankee /
on your knees . . . / scattering bonemeal for tulips" (28-29, 32),
and she declares "I will be back" (39). It is important to note
here that this "fabric" of her "first body" is often a site for the

everyday violence of the immigrant experience. The body is a canvas where she is simultaneously locked in as well as marked physiognomically as the "other." This becomes apparent in the way racial politics enters the politics of love in many of her poems. In "Two Love Poems of a Concubine" she writes:

> . . . I touch
> my Indian body lightly.
> The answer comes
> in the shape of a woman without breasts
> and holds two smooth stones in her hands
>
> *I am deformed and black*
> *and greater than your sadness* (15-21)

In "Poem (for my Father)," where the speaker addresses the eponymous figure of contention and quarrel in her poems, this longing for "reinstatement" is replicated as a longing for the "pre-immigrant" state through a second birth:

> In the first flowering of grief,
> I believed in rebirth.
> The second time the loam dries
> and the scales fall from my eyes
> I swear
> to serve the sick and hungry,
> to toil the land,
> to pray to Jesus
> and if I marry
> to marry of my own people
> and never go to America
> or if I do, to throw myself
> like a burning page
> into her rivers of oil. (88-101)

Here, the "double consciousness," the paradoxical circumstance of a brown woman's exile and its cultural implications is represented as being intertwined in a skewed survivor's guilt of having escaped the fate of "being married off at sixteen"(78), and the longing to be reinstated through "rebirth" into that fold, to "marry of my own people"(97) and to never be a *"stranger . . . in your own land / . . . to forget your own language"* (55-56). Similarly, in "Poem for Gawain," part instruction manual, part love poem addressed to her son, which stunningly brings together many of Ray's thematic concerns, she writes to her "Half-breed / child" (1-2) and transforms his second generation immigrant destiny into an allegory of her own country's "divisions, its inalterable destiny" (7):

I would like to save you,
to search for a second home.
But there is none
because we are the poor
and the elders of the earth.
So use my body as a shield and behind its metal sing
of the dark . . .   (10-17)

The sequence further explores this theme of division and reinstatement through a dazzling examination of national and cultural trauma. The historical rift created between the Hindus and the Muslims during Partition is posited as an allegory for the trauma of division inherent in the immigrant consciousness. In the second part of the poem, this metaphor extends toward love via the Aristophanes myth of the round people as described in Plato's *Symposium*. The myth states we are forever looking for the severed half of ourselves longing for a prior wholeness, a longing stemming from a recognition of an inherent "lack" when faced with the condition of eros. Shreela Ray writes in repudiation of this allegory of love in an effort to revise the premise to that of an inter-racial relationship:

> And if you should meet Aristophanes first,
> ask him,
> when a man goes in search
> of his sundered female half,
> must she be of the same race?   (38-42)

In truth, the severance that Ray suffers in migration remains impossible to recover, the struggle to be reinstated to an erstwhile wholeness or "roundness" forever left wanting by the inability to return to that "first" place. This idea of wholeness itself is located in an erotic triangulation to the condition of exile and the fantasy of a parallel, un-immigrated self, a cut branch that might've grown straight. She returns to this theme again in the fifth part of the poem, " . . . For thirteen years I have carried / dead fathers, grandfathers, uncles / and the virgin halves of myself . . . " (74-76) But this is not to say there isn't a dream of an alternate wholeness, a relinquishing of the nameless loss of exile, to finally grow roots and "make a garden out this (second) place"; a gesture toward finding a "home" where, as Naguib Mahfouz writes, "all your attempts to escape cease":

> Sometimes as we watch for the dawn
> and the paper, and I see the red and blue
> flag with its one white star
> I cut with my own hands,
> wrap itself around our makeshift staff. (101-105)

But this scene of suburban domesticity is immediately dislocated by the spectre of the Gulf war and the knowledge of her own complicity in the nation's military-industrial complex, in a dazzling collision of the personal and

the political: " . . . I am frightened. / My life is like the
wastelands / Amerika leaves behind her." (106-109) Thus,
a poem addressed to a young son doesn't devolve into a
lullaby but pivots into a warning, a manual of survival in
a warmongering nation whose people " . . . cannot be saved
from this / by nails or sabbaths or chemistry" (107-108). In
"Revolutionary," another poem addressed to her father, she
writes of this complicity and most importantly what the void
left by the severance of exile has been replaced by:

> Who installed machine guns in my eyes?
> Who turned my arms into weapons,
> for everywhere I gaze is devastation.
>
> If you send anyone with letters,
> or love or money, warn then
> beforehand, not to approach
> me face to face. Let them say
> my name in that special way,
> and touch my hair with a sign
> or flower of our country.   (4-13)

The notion of this irreparable severance brought about
by migration, and the longing toward that prior wholeness
is explored again and again in Ray's later poems. It is most
clearly dramatized in "Zero at 32," one of the two poems
written, seemingly, on the eve of her 32nd birthday. *Night
Conversations With None Other*, her only book published in
America came out in 1977 when she was 35, having lived in
the US at this point for exactly the same amount of time as
the years of her early childhood and girlhood in England and
India. In "Zero at 32," Shreela commemorates this moment:

The days of my life split
in half, and will not speak to each other.

. . .

The blind one believes
his eyes are at the back of his head.
The other leaves the country
and is thrown out of posh restaurants.

I fall asleep in the snow dreaming
that someday
they will shake hands, like two good losers
and I shall be whole again.   (1-2, 7-14)

Similarly, in "Towards a 32nd Birthday" from *Night Conversations . . .*, a scenic afternoon drive on the highway after rain merges into a dark reverie as an unnamed "you" "return(s) to redress / eight years of my grievances" (9-10), taking stock of all her roles as "foreigner," "woman," "mother," "wife," and "jongleur," an itinerant minstrel. In the last stanza, there is that same sense of arriving at a point where she can divide her life into two distinct halves, a point where she will have to cross over into a more definite exile:

The sun's waning shaft hangs above us all
like the sword of the other
archangel.
If it falls it would cut the road in half.   (28-31)

In 1977, on the event of her first book, *Night Conversations with None Other*, being disqualified for the National Book Awards on the grounds of citizenship, Shreela Ray penned a

SHREELA RAY

protest letter to the staff director explaining her reasons for not relinquishing her Indian citizenship:

" ... I came to this country having just turned eighteen, my college education is entirely American. My experiences and my language are of this (country) and its people—a nation of immigrants with whom I have spent seventeen years. I, too, am an immigrant. Although, though I am not permitted to vote, I pay taxes, and if I were a man, would have had to submit to being drafted, in order to become a citizen, I would have to repudiate the first seventeen years of my life and the land in which I was born. I can no more do that than I can repudiate these past seventeen years and the land in which I became."

I see Shreela Ray's poetics located in the contentious space between this "first" place, the country of her birth where she came of age, and the second where she became an artist and a mother and lived as a citizen of exile. The purpose of this essay is not to reduce Ray's work solely to the thematic preoccupation of self-exile. It is to show how Ray forged a poetic diction and syntactic ouvre out of this condition that is original and wholly her own. Homi Bhabha, writing in the *Times Literary Supplement* in 1978, talks about the "myth of perpetual beginnings" that he identifies in Indo-Anglian poetry, and the subsequent Indo-Anglian anxiety of writing in English in postcolonial India. Through her early migration, I suspect, Shreela unknowingly escaped that uneasy awareness of writing in the "borrowed" tongue that the poets in her country were still grappling with or were made to grapple with by nativist detractors who considered the origins of Indian English writing to be inauthentic. As Kamala Das writes in her poem, "An Introduction":

The language I speak,
Becomes mine, its distortions, its queernesses
All mine, mine alone.
It is half English, half Indian, funny perhaps, but it is
    honest,
It is as human as I am human, don't
You see?   (11-16)

Did the double estrangement of writing in English in America free Shreela Ray's linguistic sensibilities? Syntax is identity, says Li-Young Lee. Whatever violence that geographical displacement wrought on her language is evident in the sheer formal and aesthetic range and syntactic peculiarity Ray brought to her poems. The dizzying cross-referencing of eastern and western myths; the homage to other artists like Simone De Beauvoir, Nazim Hikmet, Hemant Kumar, John Berryman, Kafka; her interest in gardening and botany; the syncretism inherent in her work with an awareness of both eastern and western poetic traditions; the bright thread of religion and scripture, mythology and philosophy that runs through her work—all of it is dazzling and a mark of a poet well on her way to greatness, had the circumstances been different. Above all, even as Shreela Ray's poems begin in a state of quarrel with god, with her father, with her country, with America, they never descend into despair and always make room for the sublime, identifying love, above all else, as revolutionary:

You and I have not killed anyone.
We have not served the hungry stones,
or poisoned children . . .
   . . .
So when we walk in Highland Park . . .
   . . .

say, how could we be wrong to kiss,
first under the linden next,
the gingko next to the cottonwood?

("Antiwar," 15-17, 19, 23-25)

In a letter, not included in this anthology, written three years before her death in late '91, Ray writes to a friend, inquiring longingly after Darjeeling, "Most of all I would love to see the botanical gardens again. Of all the places now I miss that one . . . ." Thus, towards the end of her life she harkens back to the flora of Darjeeling which opens her first book. She continues, " . . . there are so many things to ask you but what I really want is to see again, to be there, to be witness, be certain of change; to know with the same but changed body the changes in the safest world I once knew." She returns to that first place, to "see again" if only in her mind the "eternal pasture folded in all thought" (Duncan 4), her life coming full circle around the garden of her exile.

Here is the book, reader. I suspect you will hear this voice and that her poems will speak as privately to you as they do to me.

....

ROHAN CHHETRI is a writer and translator. His latest book is *Lost, Hurt, Or in Transit Beautiful* (Tupelo Press / HarperCollins IN, 2021). A PhD candidate at the University of Houston, he is a recipient of a 2021 PEN / Heim grant for translation and his poems have appeared most recently in *The Paris Review* and *New England Review*.

WORKS CITED

Bhabha, Homi K.; Parthasarathy, R. "Indo-Anglican attitudes." *TLS, Times literary supplement* 3 (1978): 136.

Das, Kamala. "An Introduction." *Summer in Calcutta: Fifty Poems,* Rajinder Paul, New Delhi, 1965.

Duncan, Robert. "Often I Am Permitted to Return to a Meadow." *The Opening of the Field,* New Directions, 1987.

Ray, Shreela. Letter to Ms. Cunliffe. 29 November 1977. *Shreela Ray, On the Life and Work of an American Master. Pleiades & Gulf Coast,* 2021.

Ray, Shreela. Letter to Pedma, 1 November 1991. S Ray Letters 4. Private Archive, de Leeuw family.

Rilke, Rainer M. "Archaic Torso of Apollo." *Selected Poems of Rainer Maria Rilke,* New York: Harper & Row, 1981. Print.

Wright, James. "Lying in a Hammock at William Duffy's Farm in . . . " *Poetry Foundation,* Poetry Foundation, https://rb.gy/8wnttd

SHREELA RAY /
RADIUS TO MY ULNA

Tishani Doshi

I began reading the poems and letters of Shreela Ray in the Autumn of 2020, some months into the global coronavirus pandemic. I hadn't been able to return home to India, and Ray's ache for country resonated with mine. In a letter to her friend Sitakant in 1991, which meanders from worrying about the Gulf War to her older son's philosophy degree, she admits that she should never have come to America; that aside from her family there had been little to sustain her. "I am full of regrets. I love India and genuinely yearn for it. The blood in me goes uphill towards it. I can understand now why in earlier times exile was punishment worse than death for certain ranks of people." This longing finds its way into her poems too. In "Falling Asleep," she writes: "The closest sea is 300 miles away./ I wish I could go home, but now/ change frightens me and the language/ is not one I write in anymore."

Ray was born in the Eastern Indian state of Odisha in 1942. At 18 she flew to America to study at the Iowa Writer's Workshop, a move that would act as a kind of severance, and of which she would write: "The world has never been the same since." If you imagine the Bay of Bengal as a kind of misshapen upturned oyster, then Ray comes from the northeastern part of the oyster's circumference, while I come from the stem on the south-eastern coast of Tamil Nadu. My sea extends to mingle with the Andaman Sea and the Indian Ocean, but it shares the same temperament as Ray's. So when she writes of fish stink and fields and sunlight, the "salt-burned casuarinas," and the "one small boat/ its sails like the voice box of a gramophone," she's tapping into an intimate sea-consciousness I share.

Ray is both a poet of the sea and a poet of exile—a popular category in poetry. Whether that exile is enforced, as it was with Ovid, or self-imposed, the sea is a potent trope for the idea of return. I think of Derek Walcott for whom "the sea is History," or Elizabeth Bishop, for whom the sea is knowledge "flowing, and flown," or Pablo Neruda, for whom the sea was a kind of inheritance built into his ars poetica—"oceanic, to me who enter singing/ as if with a sword among the defenseless." For Ray the sea was requital, death, ache, rich sap, water that rushed toward and over you, water that turned you back. "The Road to Puri" begins with anticipation of approaching the sea-wet earth from the rains and the ripple of paddy fields, but then the poem swerves, and Ray declares: "Tonight/ I want to sleep with a man/ raised on dahl and rice." (I confess, the swerve is what caused this reader to shift affection towards Ray). It's as though the sea isn't enough to change her; transformation must happen through something more palpable—the body. As we move closer to the sea and the poem's end, she sees a man digging a trench by his house and it reminds her of her husband,

Hendrik, their life, which is away from here. "I see you,/ my Yankee/ on your knees . . .. your Dutch hands sifting the coarse dirt," and the poem ends with another declaration: "I will be back."

Roberto Bolaño believed all writers to be exiles because they left childhood behind, and further, because venturing into literature makes exiles of readers and writers both. He wrote about leaving Chile for Mexico in 1968 at fifteen, how while Mexico City was a territory of freedom and metamorphosis, the shadow of his native land still lingered, "in the depths of my stupid heart the certainty persisted that it was there that my destiny lay." In Bolaño's version, exile is voluntary, a writer works wherever he is, but a writer outside his country has the possibility to grow wings. Edward Said, whose work Ray would have been familiar with, believed exile to be the "unhealable rift," an "essential sadness" that can never be surmounted. "The achievements of exile are permanently undermined," he wrote, "by the loss of something left behind forever." It is into the Said category of exile that I'd place Shreela Ray.

Born into a hybrid Hindu-Christian family, she would later 'self-convert' to Islam as a protest to the racist treatment of Arabs and Islam in the US, and to exist "like a bee in the bonnet." Her son Gawain said she could be exhausting, because she had "iconoclastic, or idiosyncratic, or revolutionary views that she was not shy about revealing," and further, that "she was the embodiment of Gayatri Spivak and bell hooks before they were who they were." This spikiness comes through more in Ray's letters than her poems. She interrogates Noam Chomsky (whom she had never met), about whether the Soviet presence in Afghanistan was all that unjustified, and asks whether the "Rushdie affair" was really a free speech issue (she wrote to several people about Rushdie's fatwa). Chomsky replied respectfully that he didn't see a justification for the Soviets and he clearly saw the Rushdie issue as one of free speech. Still, you admire the ballsiness, even though you sense that her ongoing tenacity could potentially get tedious.

William Meredith, friend and peer, wrote her a kind of buck-up letter that I almost want to put up on my wall, so succinctly does it admonish self-pity and the kind of obsessive bitching that leads to bitterness. In response to her complaining about Rochester being an "intellectual wasteland and socially a disaster," he counsels, "I have never known people who complain about their locale who were not at some level dissatisfied with themselves in that locale . . . I find your response uncharacteristic of your true self—you are not a promiscuous complainer . . .. Put on your best sari and go for a walk among the beech trees with your two men and see yourself in the world's admiring eyes, then go home and write a poem."

Part of what drew me to Ray though *is* the bitchiness. She writes from a place of loss and stubbornness, ambition and recklessness. In the early part of her career there's a strain of humour with real bite, which may have intensified had things gone differently. Here she is, writing to Bill Meredith, eliciting a blurb: "I mean you may not want your name on the same page with anyone you can't stand . . .. More than three (blurbs) might be a little vulgar—like dropping names." This is a woman who named her Panasonichord word processor "Beloved" (masc.), who could rage about US foreign policy in one breath, and then ask someone to describe the February sky at dusk. And she's forthright. She has mixed feelings about V.S. Naipaul, can't get excited about Bharati Mukherjee's work and is sceptical of Peter Brook's "rainbow coalition" Mahabharata.[32] This kind of strident opinion teetering on

---

[32] Peter Brook adapted his 9 hour stage play of the Mahabharata as a 6-hour TV miniseries broadcast in three installments.

snark has always been celebrated in the enclave of "male genius." For Ray—woman of colour, immigrant of bifurcated identity, one guesses she was considered a little over the top.

Reading Ray, I wondered whether she may have thrived if she'd made a similar journey thirty years later, when the construct of her outsiderdom would have been grist rather than a continuous source of alienation. If she had not washed up in Rochester but been able to find sustenance in a cosmopolitan city. If this beauty, who was used to having a "crowd of male animals" around her at parties in Breadloaf in 1962, had not needed to be permanently hooked up to a portable tank of oxygen in 1990 for her chronic sarcoidosis. If the one book she published, *Night Conversations with None Other*, had not been withdrawn from consideration for the National Book Award because of her "resident alien" status. Regret runs through her poems and letters, a series of wishes—*I wish my children could have met yours, I wish I could go home, I feel unclean, I wish I had the courage and energy to write on other things, I wish I had the money, I wish people had not indulged me and told me I had talent, obviously I don't . . ..*

The poem I keep circling back to is "Poem (for my father)," where she writes about the "malice/ my right foot bears my left." Something about that line echoed Akhmatova's "The Song of the Last Meeting": "I pulled the glove for my left hand/ onto my right." With Akhmatova, parting is painful and awkward but there is at least an attempt to hold one with the other. It is the dissolution of an entire Russian love story concisely packed into a poem. At the end of it you sense the speaker comes off bruised, but stronger. Ray just comes off bruised. For her, parting is sure death. The poem offers little space for the restoration of beauty. "Who would want to hurt me?" she asks, after listing various possibilities of her finishing: "head in a noose of jonquils," "maybe as I step out of a car," "maybe (it is often possible)/ by my own hand."

The poem's last line does not even allow for the flicker of Akhmatova's "yellow, indifferent flame," instead, she asks for the hunter's spear a second time, a third, "until I am / my own faintest memory."

In the same poem, Ray writes about being adrift in unknown streets, "The weight of night crushes/ your chest. Radius and ulna separate." That image of those two long bones of our forearm losing their joinery and somehow being adrift, becomes my lasting image of Ray's work. This is a poet who is longing to be heard, in whatever language will have her. A poet who is so beset with estrangements, she tells her father "you should have married me off at sixteen." She swears to "pray to Jesus," "to marry of my own people." "Certainly I will forget/ all this foolishness of poetry." It is a negation of her entire American life, but perhaps only because no one was listening:

I had hoped to read to you
but my words are impaled in the silence
and only the centipedes moving
among the brown rotting flowers
hear the scream and are heedless.

I began to think of the radius and ulna as the sea and the shore, how they run parallel to each other with the illusion of meeting somewhere, and to think of Shreela Ray as the radius to my ulna in the way that we create our poetic lineages where we find connections. I too arrived in America at 18 and shared her mild horror of middle America. I too felt there was no escape from that "unbearable American benevolence." I too wrote an abundance of letters from an isolated cottage. I too once asked: "Do you mind me dropping the auntie?" (my request was not met favourably). I too obsessed about the marriage-children-freedom dilemma. I too felt the rebuff of wholeness: "The days of my life split in half and will not speak to each other." I too felt a stranger in my country but longed for my country when I was away from it; to hear film songs blaring from loudspeakers and rooftops, to eat raw mangoes with chilli and salt, for the rivers and crows, the dust and the sea.

I am a generation removed from Ray. Cheaper air travel and technology helped shrink the size of my homesickness. Ray stayed in America. I left. But even if I hadn't, it would have been impossible to write a poem like "Letter Home," its dissonance of broken beds and broken wrists, of letters that arrive sporadically about examinations and talk of marriage, and ends heartbreakingly with:

Let your letter say,
We have lost the records of your birth
and departure. Nobody
misses you in Bhubaneswar.

For all the constant mourning and oblivion that Ray addresses in her work, there is one corner of resistance that runs counter to it, that acts as a kind of hinge between radius and ulna. A fixity of pulling up earth and putting down roots. If Ray is a poet of the sea and exile, then she is also poet of the garden. Gardening for her was the highest form of civilized activity. In her letters she claims if she had to live her life over, she'd study horticulture. She was always asking people what they were growing in their gardens and telling them about hers: "The crocuses are up and the snowdrops have been around for several months . . .. I've had a steady sighting through the dreariest of months, of one or two here and there, just when everything seems so grim, or maybe I am conditioned towards thinking so because it is emblematic of hope."

The garden was a place of conversation and joy. Transplantation was not traumatic in a garden. You could take a seed from one part of the world and plant it in another. The garden was a place to putter and weed, to watch the rain fall even if your marriage was teetering. It was not just ornamental, it was useful too, like language. The garden was nourishing. "Shall I send you some seeds? Tell me what kinds?" It was a place of replenishing, integral for survival. While Virginia Woolf lay claim to a room of one's own, for Ray, the imperative was a garden. In "Night April" there's a flicker of the triumph Ray believes she might have had if she had been able to go beyond the weighing and measuring that staying involves. Ray knows she is not destined for that triumph, but she wants to make a go of it anyway: "Before I draw back my wings and fall / into the keel of birdlike flowers / by god I will make a garden of this place."

....

TISHANI DOSHI is a Welsh-Gujarati poet, novelist and dancer. Her most recent books are *Girls Are Coming Out of the Woods*, shortlisted for the Ted Hughes Poetry Award, and a novel, *Small Days and Nights*, shortlisted for the RSL Ondaatje Prize and a *New York Times* Bestsellers Editor's Choice. *A God at the Door*, her fourth collection of poems, is forthcoming in 2021. She lives in Tamil Nadu, India.

EXTENSIONS OF THE DIVINE IN SHREELA RAY'S *NIGHT CONVERSATIONS WITH NONE OTHER*

Kaitlin Rizzo

Voltas of severed limbs—corporeal, planetary, botanical, or otherwise—often end Shreela Ray's poems. Reading her first and only collection of poetry, *Night Conversations with None Other* (1977), I still don't fully understand how she makes the stench of shorn limbs—and the feeling of being sundered—smell, all at once, like flowers from childhood, like piss, and like scents I know I can never fully imagine. For example, the perfume from the Magnolia campbellii, which opens this book, grows only in Myanmar, southwestern China, and the Himalayas.

It is this tree, from the early years of Ray's life, which bears the first volta of execution in *Night Conversations*. In her opening poem, the campbellii becomes an emblem for the part of Ray she sees first severed from herself when she emigrates to America for college at eighteen. In its final lines, Ray says if the nuns back home knew what she would remember of it, standing in the courtyard of their school,

in the nights of this runaway exile . . .
the sweet, rich scent,
the cream and white . . .
eight inches across . . .   (19-22)

And here, she turns: "they would cut that tree down" (24). The conditional tense makes this an imagined execution, but as the book goes on, each severance of Ray's will risk more and more. Her body will slip further into a permanent American present, and later into her own future, after she's already passed away, as the central figure of *Night Conversations* comes to be written about by another speaker after she's been decapitated.

There is a refractory quality to these works, a prismatic effect, from the glazing and unglazing of violence through overtones of love, sex, anger, and everything in between. In "a manner of attachment," Ray flirtatiously dares her reader, coaxing them to see the nuances of this world more clearly:

Come into the sunlight before me
a little longer . . ..
or are you afraid
of the parallax
light would perform?   (1-5)

It's an eerie love poem and she doesn't answer whether her audience will walk towards the challenge. Instead, she leaves it open to every individual reading the book to decide for themselves. Ray will call her own speaker-self forward shortly after, to much greater risk, in "Poem (for my Father)." There, she meets "the Black Mother" (9), "the ferry across the ocean of existence" (11), the goddess, Kali—and puts any reader afraid of simply *looking* at a parallax, to shame.

She wears a girdle of human arms . . .
One on either side of her, her
handmaidens grin as they tear
the limbs of children, and eat.

I go closer.
I have seen her beautiful
by another name . . .

I offer you one bleeding knee,
like straws my last two hands
to add to your ten . . .
I have also known galleries
of angels and demons.
Lady of harmonies, couple
my north and south.   (13-19, 28-37)

This is so bold it bears reiterating: *she approaches a goddess whose handmaidens are currently devouring children and requests something from her.* She shows deference, even love, to Kali. And yet, there is a question in her deference because it is clear the speaker is not fully mortal herself. She offers her "*last* two hands" as tribute. This "last" implies she once had more limbs at her disposal and puts the speaker in an unknown state of corporeality from the start.

The poem's larger narrative centers around Ray's return visit to India after living in the U.S. She mentions more limbs beyond hands have gotten lost along the way, and overhears a neighbor saying, "what a disgrace . . . to forget . . . (her) own language" (2.17-2.18). The speaker promises, if she is reborn, "to marry of . . . (her) own people/ and never go to America" (2.58-2.59) These stanzas about Kali can then be read as a prayer, but it is unclear what kind of prayer. Is this a request for reentrance to Ray's once-kingdom; is it is an invocation against life in America; or is it both? Regardless, she asks Kali, with her "girdle of human arms," to couple her edges, to protect her.

By connecting with the goddess this way, Ray foreshadows the violent benevolence she will come to employ throughout rest of her book. She makes, and will continue to make, several points at once—about power, image, and divine motherhood—namely, how protection sometimes looks like a woman bathed in death.

It's important to note, with the speaker's complicated relationship to corporeality, Ray writes as someone who positions herself, not just *alongside* the feminine, violent divine—but somehow *within* it. Though poems like Sylvia Plath's "Lady Lazarus" immediately come to mind from the 1960s, by the 70s, when *Night Conversations* comes out, this positioning of the self *within* the feminine, violent, yet benevolent, divine still feels like a rare tradition that's being reborn as Ray writes into it. It's even rarer when you consider she fuses Eastern and Western themes to do so. She weaves together references of her son Gawain, her husband Henrik, Queen Zenobia, Hemant Kumar, Mahmoud Darwish, William Meredith, and many others, as if trying to conjure all her beloveds into a realm which is safe.

As is typical of trailblazers, it is easier to compare Ray's poetics to the work of the generation that follows her. For example, "Daughter-Mother-Maya-Seeta" by Reetika Vazirani provides a foothold. Vazirani's title implies the kind of allegorical mind-work Ray traffics in, although Ray more explicitly explores these relationships within the body of her poems than Vazirani, who predominantly uses titles to facilitate the link. "Lullaby," particularly echoes some of Ray's most unnerving lines to her son. Vazirani's "Lullaby" reads,

I would not sing you to sleep.
I would press my lips to your ear
and hope the terror in my heart stirs you.

Ray's "Poem for Gawain" is the most salient to compare
for our purposes here because it's one of two poems explicitly
titled after Ray's son. It also references her desire to likewise
write her child some form of lullaby. However, there are
many themes in *Night Conversations* worthy of comparison
with Vazirani's larger body of work which will benefit from
further scholarship in the future. In "Poem for Gawain,"
Ray writes,

This casket, this body,
lie on it,
warm, familiar,
as though you were in your own room,
in your own bed . . .

I will write this story for you
on a tortoise shell comb,
where the song becomes
something old and slow and hidden
in the carapace of your tiny
mortality . . .

Learn American-English
live long
and be strong
and gun your mother down . . .   (1.19-1.23, 3.9-
                                                      3.14, 4.4-4.7)

And then, the final stanza:

I cannot tell you enough
that I am frightened . . .
My life is like the wastelands
Amerika leaves behind her.
And a people cannot be saved . . .
when every new infant is cradled
in the jawbone of an ass
bleached in that desert.   (6.25-6.33)

When readers first look at "Lullaby," it may be difficult,
at first, not to reduce the "carapace of (Vazirani's son's) tiny
mortality" solely to the tragic biography of Vazirani's murder-
suicide in 2003. However, within the poem, Vazirani makes no
reference to how exactly she wants the "terror in (her) heart"
to stir her baby's, thus leaving it open to interpretation. What
is certain about the poem is only: the speaker wishes terror
to be communicable, and she hopes this communication will
provoke some kind of kindred response in the next generation.
It is possible, like Ray, Vazirani is cultivating her son's societal
resistance and is spurred to do so in reaction to a violently
discriminatory America. The line, "I would not sing you to
sleep," by virtue of its negation, implies a shadow-self: *I would
sing you awake.*

Rather than seeking to reflect her own fear in her son, as
Vazirani does, Ray advises him to,

use (her) body as a shield
. . . sing
of the dark
so when death comes
you will think it is the sea.   (1.15-1.18)

Like her counterpart, Ray is not afraid of broaching
frightening subjects with her child, even when these subjects

are about his death or her own terror of American hegemony. But the difference between Ray and Vazirani is Ray tries to insulate Gawain from the natural fear-response which results. Poem-to-poem, how Ray tries to protect Gawain changes, but the underlying sense of her channeling Kali does not. In "Notes from the Near East," Ray tells the audience, "Gawain has hurt no one" (2.44). She "smoke(s) (the gods) out/ in bathrooms . . . where (she) locks herself" (2.53-2.56), trying to protect him. She calls herself "victim and terrorist/ in equal parts" ("Address before an Empty Assembly," [11-12]). In "Asia," she doesn't try to save a boat full of people drowning, but "conduct(s) (them)/ to the vaults of (her) memory . . ./ beyond contempt and further violations" (12-16). Ray most consistently underlines some complex version of the idea that "if (her) . . . redemption requires the death of one other/ or six others, . . . (she) insist(s) on being damned" ("Address before an Empty Assembly," [2.8-2.11]). A notable exception to this is in "From a Willow Cabin," where she says, "the night passes me on to disbelief/ and belief in the mercy of killing/ them or me" (69-71) but she immediately iterates: she has already watched, "the orange flicker jammed in (her) . . . breast, smoke out" (73-75), so there is some sad degree of futility to this speech of understandable survivalism.

She is still alive and still fighting at the end of "Poem for Gawain." She suggests, for safety, her son radically assimilate into the U.S. To "live long/ and be strong," he should, "learn American-English." This sounds like something a mother might say to her son as he's running out the door on his way to school. She follows her command with rote clichéd invocations, the kind of offhand wishes someone might make in a marriage toast, to systematically un-prepare readers for the coming volta. She lulls them into these gentle abstractions, before she concretely flat-lines, telling Gawain: "gun your mother down."

While the reality of Vazirani's tragedy hangs over "Lullaby," there is typically an inversion of this immolation impulse in Ray. Ray's work most often self-reflexively visits the consequences of her own death drive unto herself. But this particular poem ends in the metaphorical death of both Ray *and* her son. In the final stanza, she refutes Job 24:5, which says, "as wild asses in the desert, go they forth to their work; rising betimes for . . . prey: the wilderness yieldeth food for them and their children." She morphs this utopic vision of bounty-through-work into an anti-capitalistic stance, saying,

a people cannot be saved . . .
when every new infant is cradled
in the jawbone of an ass
bleached in that desert."   (6.25-6.33)

In the section prior, she iterated,

"graveyards have no entry
for Marxists poets . . ..
so I buried them all
in my head   (5.15-5.18)

thus further promoting an anti-capitalistic reading of her last lines. The metaphor of Ray, as an ass "bleached" in the desert of America, also implies the violence of white supremacy through capitalism, which often results in overworking women of color until death.

This book, and its publication history, follows a sadly similar Orphic arch. The limbs of Ray's life, professionally and otherwise, keep severing. She moves through elegies and absences, before coming to some degree of acceptance with her own premature end. She reflects back on her early life, and uplifts sisterhood, "In Praise of the Beauty of

Asian Women." This reads, in some way, like support for all the South Asian American women who begin publishing in the U.S. shortly after Ray breaks the glass ceiling. In her final poem, "Address before an Empty Assembly," Ray foreshadows the next seventeen years of her life, before her eventual death of Sarcoidosis in 1995 at the early age of fifty-two.

Echoing the momentary third-person alienation of "gun your mother down," she amplifies her growing depersonalization by using the third-person for most of "Address before an Empty Assembly." She writes, "Mohammad Darweesh,/ I want to see . . . your picture on the front page of the APR" (3.23-3.25). But a voice-over quickly cuts in. "She was sounding dangerous./ She couldn't find a job/ and her poems returned with greater frequency" (3.26-3.28). At one point, Ray depersonalizes to such an extent she ironically assumes the avatar "Olga Volga," a Russian woman who serves to mirror Ray's experience of America. Olga ventriloquizes for Ray, saying a suppression tactic of the KGB is to "make one . . . unheard of" (4.15-4.17)—underscoring the suppression of Ray's career. Ray does this, in part, to also point out the hypocrisy of a PEN ad which appears within the work as well. It says, "members pledge to oppose any form of suppression . . . in the country to which they belong" (4.1-4.5).

Ray replies: "you've got to be in a non-Western country" (4.9-4.10) for PEN to take notice, implying Western countries tend to see oppression as a non-Western problem. The poem's speaker then gaslights and diminutizes Ray in response: "poor girl . . . 5 years of shrinks too" (4.27). The work doesn't say how she dies, but suggests the building violence had something to do with it by virtue of this line's position at the end of the penultimate section. In the poem's final part, the speaker immediately flips into the past tense. The remaining end of "Assembly" speaks to Ray's life-after-death:

11 years now she's been dead . . .

I buried her in two pieces . . .
her terrorist western head
is in the front yard
among the English daisies . . .

Her victim body is rendered to dust
in the back under the hibiscus . . .

She sings at the top of her shrill
voice ragas for morning and evening.   (5.1-5.10,
                                              5.18-5.19)

Ray's status of unknown divine origin feels, at first,
as if it's resolved in these final moments. She invokes the
echo of herself as the demi-god and first poet claimed by
the Western cannon, Orpheus. It's an adept comparison; she
bears a similar position in the U.S. cannon, given she is, as
Kazim Ali writes, the "first widely read and widely published
South Asian American poet" (103) in the country. Here, she
reimagines Orpheus as the primary source of severance for
her once-unified whole. In describing the pieces of herself as
a "terrorist western head" and a "victim body . . . rendered
to dust," Ray implies the source of disconnect from her
Eastern body is the result of the violent dominion of Western
thought—which found its hold over Ray through poetry. Still,
she descents from this dominion and re-complicates her own
divinity by using her "terrorist western head" to sing ragas
"no one listens (to) . . . or understands" (5.20), except the
speaker of the poem. For them, Ray writes so they

    will not
    forget (their) name and what (they) are

or from where (they came), and go
inhuman
mad
not knowing.   (5.23-5.27)

Ray operates in a similar protective capacity for the speaker as she had for Gawain. The implication: she feels the need to protect others from being pushed beyond the bounds of their own humanity, the way she was pushed beyond the bound of her own. Now that she has no Eastern body to protect anyone with anymore, she uses the only tool she has left: the music in her decapitated, chthonic head—and her spell *holds*. The speaker remembers and the audience reading her book listens.

Night Conversations took Shreela Ray thirteen years to finish (Ray 11/26/77), and when the National Book Award committee requested it for review, they realized she wasn't a citizen and refused to consider it under the award's citizenship bylaws. By then, Ray had lived in this country for seventeen years. She'd learned from Charles Olsen (Ray 11/26/91), William Meredith, John Berryman, Robert Frost, and many others (Ray 8/2/62)—and most importantly, her book still resonates as it did then, almost fifty years from its original publication date.

But in the eyes of the National Book Award Committee, she had to be a citizen. To do this, Ray would've had to, as she tells them in a letter, give up her Indian citizenship, to "repudiate the first seventeen years of . . . (her) life and the land in which . . . (she) was born. (She) . . . could no more do that than . . . repudiate the past seventeen years (of her life in the U.S.) and the land in which . . . (she) became" (11/29/77).

The National Book Award Committee, in this moment, makes itself forever inextricable from the severance prophesized by Ray in "Address to an Empty Assembly;" they empty the room. It seems Ray had, in characteristic fashion, already put her finger to the pulse of what was happening in her life when she composed the end of *Night Conversations*. Ray would never again publish another full-length collection. Though she kept writing and submitting her work, the lack of resources and communal support on the institutional level only amplified as Ray grew older. April 11th 1991, she writes a letter to Gawain referring to herself as both "perpetrator" and "victim." Though the letter is written fourteen years after the publication of *Night Conversations*, this still feels reminiscent of the dichotomy between her "terrorist western head" and her "victim body." She says,

> I wish now . . . people had not indulged me and told me I had talent. Obviously I don't . . . There is no reason why you should make the same mistakes I made. Now looking back, I see my life a gigantic hoax in which I am the main victim and perpetrator. You can imagine what that does to my self esteem and hope in life . . . I love you very much Gawain.

Some measure of the accountability that belonged to other people and institutions, it seems, psychologically inverted. That Shreela Ray ever felt compelled to write she was untalented, that she'd wasted her life on mediocre poetry, that these are the words an extraordinary poet sends her son in 1991, just three years before her death—was avoidable. To this day, the National Book Award website says they still require applicants to be citizens, be the process of seeking citizenship, or else be legally barred from doing so.

Hers is a legacy which requires much grappling with from American institutions. Ray wrote her last line, talking about her friends, on August 12th or 13th of 1994 from a hospital: "great crossings in the dark desert." In this, she seemingly recovers the darkness from the white sands at the end of "Poem for Gawain." But it is "Notes from the East," which most reads like a prescription for Ray's reclamation in the poetic cannon. She inquires, as if asking after herself, "whatever happened to Zenobia, self-styled Queen of the East?," and answers,

> the sand in your eye
> was once part of her . . .
>
> If it is part of her brain,
> you will go mad . . .
> If it is a scrap of her heart,
> there is no knowing what may happen.
> In any case,
> give it to the boy
> and he will plant it in a place of honour
> in the potter's field.   (87-101)

I found this towards the beginning of *Night Conversations*, but I originally missed Ray's implication of interpersonal invocation and dissociation here. I've since learned there are many versions of Queen Zenobia's life scattered through history (Talhami 353). The essentials are this: Queen Zenobia marries the Roman citizen who rules her homeland in what is today Syria. After her husband's death, she attempts to free her people from Western tyranny. What happens next is where the stories diverge: by some accounts, the Queen poisons herself when it is clear reconquest is imminent. Other sources say, the conquerors drag her to Rome as an exhibition of their triumph. She is later allowed to live in the land of exiles in Tivoli, where she is forever cut off from her Syrian homeland.

Both versions contain something of Shreela Ray in them. The first, sources her immolation instinct. The second, hints at how Ray married into a land intent on othering her, a place which simultaneously then comes to occupy and belong to her. In "Notes from the East," Shreela Ray reminds us the pieces of herself she leaves behind are still reactive, still fighting, and they're making their way back to us through the dark desert. May we see this generation plant them in a place of honor indeed.

....

KAITLIN RIZZO is a writer, researcher, and translator on Artemisia Gentileschi. Born and raised in Florida, she currently lives in Texas where she is the assistant editor for *Gulf Coast's* Online Poetry Exclusives and a Master's candidate in the University of Houston's Creative Writing Program.

WORKS CITED

Ali , Kazim. "Shreela Ray: An Introduction." *New England Review,* vol. 41, no. 1, 2020, pp. 103–113.

Plath, Sylvia. *The Collected Poems.* Edited by Ted Hughes, HarperPerennial Modern Classics, 2018.

Ray, Shreela. Letter to Bill and Jean. 26 November 1991. *Shreela Ray, On the Life and Work of an American Master. Pleiades & Gulf Coast,* 2021.

Ray, Shreela. Letter to Ms. Cunliffe. 29 November 1977. *Shreela Ray, On the Life and Work of an American Master. Pleiades & Gulf Coast,* 2021.

Ray, Shreela. Letter to Gawain. 11 April 1991. *Shreela Ray, On the Life and Work of an American Master. Pleiades & Gulf Coast,* 2021.

Ray, Shreela. Letter to Kunti. 14 February 1991. *Shreela Ray, On the Life and Work of an American Master. Pleiades & Gulf Coast,* 2021.

Ray, Shreela. Note in Hospital. 12 or 13 August 1994. *Shreela Ray, On the Life and Work of an American Master. Pleiades & Gulf Coast,* 2021.

Ray, Shreela. Letter to Miki. 2 August 1962. *Shreela Ray, On the Life and Work of an American Master. Pleiades & Gulf Coast,* 2021.

Ray, Shreela. *Night Conversations with None Other.* Dustbooks, 1977.

Talhami, Ghada. *Historical Dictionary of Women in the Middle East and North Africa,* Scarecrow Press, 2012. ProQuest Ebook Central, https://ebookcentral.proquest.com/lib/uh/detail. action?docID=1144296. pp. 353.

Vazirani, Reetika. *World Hotel.* Copper Canyon Press, 2002.

SHREELA RAY:
A TESTAMENT AGAINST FORGETTING

Vandana Khanna

As a child growing up in Virginia, one of the few ties I had back to India, the country of my birth, were the faded blue aerogrammes from my grandfather that arrived every couple of months. He wrote to me faithfully over several years about the goings-on in his corner of Delhi: the lemons ripening in his garden, the Indian tennis player we both followed, a distant cousin's elaborate wedding celebration. In return, he'd ask me to write back about life in America—about school friends and neighbors that he'd met only once on his sole trip to visit us, a decade into our immigration. My grandmother, who spoke only a few words of English, words that didn't fully express the complexities of our relationship (*sick, hungry, home*) would find other ways to communicate with me. Occasionally, I'd find a small packet of raw sugar that she'd tucked into the blue folds of my grandfather's letters. The brown crystals, so different from the white, "American" sugar I was used to, added a little sweetness to the words, a balm against the despair that came from spending most of our lives apart from each other. I would put the granules on my tongue, and for a moment, let the sweetness flood my mouth with a sense of longing so strong I imagined it collapsing time and space until I was back with them again. Every letter over those many years of writing was not only a means of bearing witness to our connection, but a talisman of sorts, to guard against forgetting—my family, the stories that bound us to each other, the country from where I came.

Reading Shreela Ray's poems and letters is like having a bit of home dissolving on my tongue, a far-off sweetness from an all-too-distant past. Her work is a testament against forgetting, strengthening the ties between her and a new generation of writers who also grapple with notions of immigration, alienation, and belonging. Ray's work registers on many levels of craft—syntactically, imagistically, but perhaps what's most striking, is the ability it has to inhabit this precarious space of the "in between," describing a life of divided loyalties, of new traditions and old alliances, where nothing is just simple sweetness. In her poems, the imagery of immigration is often coupled with sharp details that feature a bite of homesickness, politics, and a sense of melancholy. Throughout her career, Shreela Ray lays bare these complex emotions with blunt, incisive observations as in her poem, "Falling Asleep," where the speaker is both literally and metaphorically "displaced":

The closest sea is 300 miles away.
I wish I could go home, but now
changes frighten me and the language
is not one I write in anymore.

Here the fears of a speaker caught between countries, languages, and identities, who questions her place in a shifting landscape, are delivered in sparse, emphatic lines. The unfiltered expression of longing, the guilt for leaving behind a native language is expressed in straightforward, unwavering statements. This is a perceptive speaker who doesn't turn away from uncomfortable truths, from the disillusionment that is often a by-product of immigration. She examines the complex negotiations a person caught "in between" countries must make— of what is given up, taken away, left behind; the accumulation of loss upon loss, with an unyielding and bold inspection.

Shreela Ray's work exhibits the kind of modern assemblage of opposing forces seen in contemporary poetry: a combination of the global and the domestic, of geopolitical concerns grounded in the personal, in the very dirt of her father's garden; the individualism of America juxtaposed with the trees, the soil, the collective air of India:

> We have ten miles to go
> when I decide
> I don't want to go back to America
> or to change the fabric
> of my first body.
> > Tonight
> I want to sleep with a man
> raised on dahl and rice.

Thus, her poems, her reflections of a life lived in one country while longing for another, becomes a study in imperfect nostalgia, asking questions that echo through many of our own minds—where is my homeland? Where do I belong? Just as the speaker in one of her later poems, "North Wind," reflects starkly, without literary flourish or pretense, upon this dilemma of alienation from one's own homeland:

But what's the point of all this now?
To whom was I calling,

"Wait for me,
wait for me"? To whom promising,
"I'll be back. You'll see"?

In one of Shreela Ray's letters written towards the end of her life, when she is ill and knows she cannot make it back to India, she expresses her longing in such vivid detail, that we get a clear picture of the price that her immigration has cost her: "I ache for India and am afraid that I shall never see her again. Never see my old aunts . . . My mother, you, just the river, the dust. The cows, and eat raw mangos with salt and chilies . . .. That I will never hear film songs blaring out of cars with loudspeakers affixed on top, a cricket match." Her nostalgia for home is reminiscent of my parents' own recollections of by-gone days, of an India frozen in time, space, and memory. This same nostalgia gifted to me, their daughter, the poet, who is tasked with remembering, with holding on tightly to a homeland that has changed, become unrecognizable. Their nostalgia so thick at times, it coated our tongues like the slick, honeyed sweetness of jalebis and found their way into my poems, layered in the lines, rooted in some of the same kinds of images Ray's letter describes.

Her wish to never have left India echoes my parents' voices in the early years of our immigration. Life was hard in America, a fact I could see so plainly, even as a child—long hours at low-paying jobs, living in a cramped one-bedroom apartment in government housing. It was easy to see why my parents longed for the home that was the India of their past, with its familiar smells and sounds—sputtering three-wheelers and crooning vegetable vendors, afternoon tea in my grandfather's walled garden, all of it offering some measure of comfort. But nostalgia can be dangerous, feeding on our expectations, tempting us to crystallize experiences into sensations that are frozen in our memories, never allowed to evolve or disappoint. These memories have to withstand great pressure to perform, dependent on things staying fixed and immovable. Shreela Ray recognizes the peril of relying on nostalgia to fill the void that immigration leaves behind in her poem, "First Mail: Delhi to Rochester," where the speaker goes back to her childhood home, reminiscing about a world where everything has changed, even the exchange rate of the rupee:

"When I was ten
I lived in Delhi on Akbar road,
near Nehru's house.
In those days
a dollar was worth 4,78 rupees."

Thus, the same struggles and fears that Shreela Ray first wrote about over 40 years ago feel just as current and pertinent today, with Ray doing the hard work of representation by being one of the earliest Asian American writers to appear widely in prominent publications. Even as she is relatively unknown by many contemporary Asian American poets, myself included, only having come across her work now, this many years into my own writing career, I recognize the impact of her writing and publishing had on the literary landscape. Ray is a foremother in our communal poetic lineage. She held the door open for the rest of us—by writing, publishing, being a presence in workshops and at readings, often as the only Asian American in the room—refusing to disappear, refusing to give up on her art even in the face of illness, discrimination, and disregard. The thread between Shreela Ray and the rest of us is long and tenacious, one that gets thicker and more resilient each day a new AAPI writer publishers her work, sits in a workshop, gives a reading. For when we say representation matters, this is a prime example. A reader has only to flip through this book, spend just a little bit of time to recognize the undeniable quality to Ray's observations and use of language, the seamless blending of the personal and the political, the unflinching examination of the repercussions of immigration on an individual, that still resonate with contemporary writers and readers.

Shreela Ray's work is emblematic of language and imagery put to use in service of a greater understanding of the sweet and the melancholy that the contributes to the immigrant experience. She is a poet who is caught between lands, languages, and labels—"Foreigner/ woman/ mother/ wife," one who is in constant "search for friendly ground" where she can "make a garden" out of the wasteland. Her work gives voice to the fear of so many who have made the journey from one homeland to another, that "We have lost the records of your birth/ and departure. Nobody misses you . . ." In one of her later letters to a friend, Ray speaks of arrangements for her death, planning to have her poems translated into her mother tongue, to have them read "through the streets down to the river. What survives beyond the longing, the loss are the words strung together on a line, someone holding a torch up to the page, someone who "sings/ for me, so I will not/ forget my name and what I am/ from where I came . . ." We who follow in Shreela Ray's footsteps will continue to hold the light up to her words and sing them from our shores. Her legacy gives us the resolve to make our own words and have them echo across thousands of miles to our homelands, so that we too, might be remembered.

....

VANDANA KHANNA is a writer, educator, and editor born in New Delhi, India. She is the author of two collections of poetry and her work has appeared widely in publications such as the Academy of American Poets' Poem-a-Day, *The New Republic*, *New England Review*, and *Guernica*. She is a poetry editor at the *Los Angeles Review*.

I WILL MAKE A GARDEN OF THIS PLACE: LETTERS TO SHREELA RAY

Alicia Jo Rabins

Dear Shreela Ray,

Though I did not know you, and my life is quite different from yours, I feel we are connected.

Some things we have in common: We are both poets and mothers. We share a love of the Mysteries. We both choose to spend our days with our hands in the dirt—both the dirt of words and literal dirt, and a scholarly streak, but we are not scholars, lacking the temperament for the academy. In our respective youths, we each stood on the same porch on the same mountain in Vermont, at Bread Loaf. Based on your letters I garnered nowhere near the attention you did.

I believe that words are the closest we limited beings get to transcending time and space. Yours grabbed me by the throat. (That's a compliment, to be clear.) My hope here is to illuminate four aspects of the world you build in words, as a person turns on a light in a room. I don't want to summarize you, to assess you from the outside; rather I feel drawn to writing you letters. And so here they are, four letters to you (plus this introduction). Garden plots seeded by your words. Quilts sewn from your words and bound by mine.

This is my first time writing a letter to a person I've not met. I'm sure I've gotten some things wrong; for that I apologize.

With love,
AJR

1. "THE MATRIARCH OF THE CLOSET POETS OF THE WORLD" (POEMS & PLANTS)

Dear Shreela,

I love reading your words about your garden. There, I feel you as the creating-and-tending-Goddess. As powerful as any divinity, and as fallible.

> I have a white wisteria which I am training as a tree, but don't have the heart to cut it back when I should, so it is quite free forming. I have made many mistakes in plant selections. A plant chosen for its colour turns out to have large coarse leaves which take up way too much space in my small plot.

Gardening is a welcome contrast to our labor as poets, in which we are not at all godlike. At least not if we care about career, which I notice you do.

We picked the wrong kind of garden for us. It's the kind that looks informal or English (why do they get credit for everything—but perhaps mine is a little anarchistic, me being Indian. In fact I'm quick to point out, it looks like an Indian miniature). But one has to labour hard to give that careless effect. Another friend has a formal Japanese style garden requiring little maintenance, once it has been laid.

Poetry and gardening are similar in the way they express culture and inhabit genre, in the way we let flow the human impulse to beautify, organize, labor. But the similarity ends there.

If, after God created the world, God then had to compete with a thousand other Gods and *their* worlds to find a slot where that world might fit; if the chances of finding such a slot were higher if God massaged the egos of those who managed those slots; if, even after finding a home for the world, God had to hustle to keep that world in existence and (unlikely) maybe even get some royalties or respect for it—well, then poets would be like God.

Gardening must be the highest form of civilized activity I know. The idea of actually taking a seed from one part of the world to another, of planning and design, colour and size for the end simply being for human pleasure. Does it redeem our bloodthirsty natures somewhat?" (*all 3 previous excerpts—letter of 14/2/91, to Kunti*)

The solitary nature of poetry is a deception; unlike gardening, it is a social game, and bloodthirsty as all social games are. You have to know how to smile, which parties to attend, which powerful people to purr near, egos to stroke, feathers to spread at opportune moments, poetry peacocks wandering the gardens of the cathedral, waiting to be chosen. And most of the time we are not chosen.

Who is published, who reviewed? Who is not? Who is considered a better writer than they actually are? Who brilliant and overlooked? *Would you be willing to read my manuscript and write a blurb?* we write. *I understand if you're too busy. We write, Thank you for considering.*

> She was sounding dangerous.
> She couldn't find a job
> and her poems returned with greater frequency.
> —SR, *Address Before an Empty Assembly*

On top of this, you certainly encountered unfairness, as a woman of color (I'm sorry, I know how you dislike being categorized) in the poetry world of the 70's, as well as a person who could clearly be a bit prickly. William Meredith wrote to you about what he acknowledged was a "monstrous injustice" (now lost to history, I believe, but I imagine it was writing-related):

> . . . [Y]ou are being bent out of shape by an event which it may turn out you will do best to rise above. I mean it. Your letter lacks the wisdom and self-assurance that is what makes yourself and your poetry so beautiful. That's why I am so distressed for you, more at your response to this monstrous injustice than at the injustice itself.
> *Letter to Shreela Ray from Bill Meredith, June 7th, 1974*

I don't know how you responded to this response to your response to this lost injustice, but I do know that a few years later, another injustice occurs. The National Book Award

committee, you find out, intended to nominate your book—
but "could" or would not since you did not hold American
citizenship. This, although you'd lived, since age eighteen,
in this land, for which you'd left your other land, in which
you'd birthed and raised two American children.

Dear Shreela, how devastating that must have been for you.
In one moment you are told you have finally won entry to the
poetry pageant—the next it is yanked away for the farthest
thing from poetry, the pedantics of bureaucracy, of borders
and passports. I imagine the committee saw this policy as
regrettable but not xenophobic. You, however, characteristically
see through the surface to the core unfairness beneath.

In your letter protesting the decision, you write:

> I came to this country having just turned eighteen, my
> college education is entirely American. My experiences
> and my language are of this and its people—a nation of
> immigrants with whom I have spent seventeen years.
> I too, am an immigrant. Although though [sic] I am
> not permitted to vote, I pay taxes, and if I were a man,
> would have had submit to being drafted, in order to
> become a citizen, I would have to repudiate the first
> seventeen years of my life and the land in which I was
> born. I can no more do that than I can repudiate these
> past seventeen years and the land in which I became.
> (Letter to Ms Cunliffe, 29 November, 1977)

From my perch in the future, I can tell you that you are not alone.

Thirty years from the date of your letter, a group of poet-
activists called Undocupoets will take up the fight you begin
here. They will succeed in persuading many of the poetry

prizes to drop the (irrelevant, exclusionary-bordering-on-racist) citizenship requirement.

I suppose I hope this means things are getting better, at least a little. The world is still not built for us.

But it speaks to us, calls to us, and we call back. We have to.

And we turn it into poems and gardens.

> Before I draw back my wings and fall
> into the keel of birdlike flowers
> by god I will make a garden of this place.
> —*"Night in April"*

Respectfully, from my garden to yours,
AJR

2. "WHAT THE SPRINGS OF MY BODY GENERATE": (MOTHER, DAUGHTER)

Dear Shreela,

Some mothers separate their mother-ness from their writer-ness. You, however, are ahead of your time in your willingness to excavate this particular geological feature of human experience.

> My wrists
> have opened and closed four times
> so I could see what the springs
> of my body generate.
> —*Poem (for my father)*

Today it's not unusual for mother-poets to proudly claim the experience. But in the 1960's and 70's, when being a woman was rare enough for "great living" poets—I think of all those men you mention as mentors from your Bread Loaf summer at age twenty, all men—unapologetically inhabiting motherhood-identity in your work is one more step away from the established model. Not that other poets didn't write about motherhood (Plath, Sexton, Rich). But you write so directly, so

> Body of boy,
> body of leaf which first
> turned and broke
> in Fall—
> something of me
> I love
> glorious brown, human body,
> demi-savage, pagan, gentile.
> That you know
> all of this
> is enough.
> —*For Gawain in November, 1975*

Is it presumptuous to write you, an elder, like this—as one mother to another? Forgive me if so. I take comfort from a letter you wrote to an auntie as you transitioned to her equal in your own eyes:

> "My dear Kunti, Do you mind my dropping the auntie? I'm too old to be calling you that. Besides, I may have acquired some wisdom along the way." (14/2/91)

With this borrowed chutzpah I observe how your letters radiate with love for your two sons. Gawain and Kabir, your sons: when you write about them, a fierce luminosity settles into your prose, like a bird on a branch.

I know this feeling, or something like it, from my own mothering. That odd, animal combination of passion and detachment. To be mother-bird, observing from above. You observe your child, while observing yourself as mother.

> [Kabir] is wonderful and is kind to me. Kinder than I am to him. (*letter, 22/3/91*)

And in this observing you witness terror, of loss, of the vastness of these cycles, which repeat in and through our small frail bodies. On the occasion of your older son Gawain's graduation, you write:

> I am experiencing a deep terror and ache realizing this is truly the end. We have no power over him anymore, to retrain or let go, because even that last is not in our power but is in the indifferent way of the world. The terror is what I have known myself to do, i.e. I hope he never leaves me in the way I left so dramatically, so thoroughly, everything I loved and [that] knew, or thought it did, me. (*letter, 22/3/91*)

Daughter as mother, mother as daughter. A Mobius strip of love and obligation and failings and the possibility of healing, even if only through forgiveness.

> I am not a model wife and mother god knows but I do try and pray that my children will learn quickly to forgive my failings. In spite of the lifelong strain I have had with my mother, I am beginning to appreciate that she could not have found me a model daughter. I wish I could make it up to her. (*letter, 22/3/91*)

Now it is time for me to confess something. I've met your son Kabir a couple times, though only briefly. He is a friend of my sister's from college. It doesn't give me any insight into your heart, but don't you think it means something, on the mystical plane, that we have touched however barely in this earthly one?

Or does it not matter, since we have words? Love letters to our children, apologies to our mothers, songs for strangers in our "tiny mortality."

> I will write this story for you
> on a tortoise shell comb,
> where the song becomes
> something old and slow and hidden
> in the carapace of your tiny
> mortality.
> —Poem for Gawain

Yours among the overlapping cycles,
Alicia Jo Rabins

3.   "THE BLOOD IN ME GOES UPHILL": EXILE

Dear Shreela,

Palpable in your letters is the pain of exile.

> I ache for India and am afraid that I shall never see her again. Never see my old aunts . . .. My mother, you, just the river, the dust. The cows, and eat raw mangos with salt and chilies and borr koli, akkhu adi. That I will never hear film songs blaring out of cars with loudspeakers affixed on top." (*letter of 21/3/91*)

I cannot pretend to understand your pain. Still, I know the taste, know how it feels to have home be thousands of miles from the place that feels most like home—not because we were forced out, but because of decisions we made. One year grows into twenty, and we've grown a whole life far from where we started, and we can't get back.

> I am full of regrets. I love India and genuinely yearn for it. The blood in me goes uphill towards it. I can understand now why in earlier times exile was punishment worse than death for certain ranks of people. Although no one has imposed exile on me, my circumstances including now my health have made it impossible for me to return or to travel anywhere. (*letter of 22/3/91*)

As you know from your life as a gardener, transplanting works. But as you know from your human experience, it is not easy to leave the land of one's youth. I confess I wanted to slap William Meredith for writing so dismissively of (and to) your broken heart.

> "Rochester for me has been an intellectual wasteland and socially a disaster," you write. I find that self-pitying. I have never known people who complain about their locale who were not at some level dissatisfied with themselves in that locale. I am not defending Rochester, although I expect it could be defended, but saying that I find your response uncharacteristic of your true self— you are not a promiscuous complainer. (*Meredith's letter of June 7th, 1974*)

I don't blame your mentor, not really. He couldn't understand; he was, must have been, at home where he was. And who knows what you wrote to him. Whatever it was, it could not have contained the raw, aching detail of your communication with friends and relatives in India, I think—who could read these words and not feel compassion?

> Please write and tell me about India. Pretend that you are speaking to someone who has never been there. How does the day begin? Is it raining. What is it like when it doesn't rain. And what do you see or hear when you look out the window / don't tell me about the well-off Indians only. Tell me about the people who work for you in your own house; what are their names? Are they fat or thin? Do they have children? How many and where do they go to school? And what do they dream about. Tell them something nice about me. Tell your cook for instance that you had a friend once who went away to the US and is very unhappy and longs for Indian food such [as] she/he would make and if he would please give me a recipe. (*letter of 21/3/9x (91?)*)

The experience of exile, even a relatively comfortable exile, is paradoxical.

It is an experience of loss, an attenuation of the self, as you beautifully capture in your poem "letter home": "We have lost the records of your birth and departure. Nobody misses you."

At the same time, the pain is a richness, like all pain it becomes an indelible part of who we are. I think of the Babylonian exile of the Jews, beginning in 586 BCE. During this time, many scholars believe the Hebrew Bible was redacted, the Hebrew alphabet finalized, and the prophecy of Ezekiel written.

Out of exile comes pain, and also poetry.

Yours in longing,
Alicia Jo Rabins

4. "THE ESSENCE OF THINGS CALL ME SISTER": PROPHECY

Dear Shreela,

Your words are those of a prophet.

> "I will not come to terms . . . never take my eyes off and retreat."—SR

It is never easy, I think, being a prophet.

I mean prophecy in the Biblical sense—not prediction of what's to come, rather an incisive castigation of present injustice.

Reading your words, I thought of this story from the Talmud, and wanted to share it with you.

It begins, like so many Jewish stories, with an argument. Rabbi Shimon bar Yochai is a mystic and ascetic living in ancient Roman Palestine. He argues with a colleague who praises the public works projects of the Romans: public markets, bathhouses, bridges. "Everything they established, they established only for their own purposes," counters Rabbi Shimon. "Marketplaces—to place sex workers in them. Bathhouses—to pamper themselves. Bridges—to collect taxes from those who pass over them."

When this critique reaches the emperor, he sentences Rabbi Shimon to death. R. Shimon goes into hiding with his son, Rabbi Elazar.

His wife brings the pair food for a time, risking her own life, until R. Shimon grows worried that she will reveal his location if tortured, because "women are easily impressionable." The two men secretly move locations to hide in a cave, where they live off a miraculous carob tree and spend their days studying Torah while buried in sand up to their necks, preserving their clothes for their thrice-daily prayers.

When the Emperor dies, and the death sentence is lifted, the two rabbis emerge. But when they see people working in the fields, rather than devoting themselves to sacred study, they are horrified. "These people abandon eternal life and occupy themselves with temporary things!" Rabbi Shimon cries, and the two begin to burn the fields around them with their eyes, simply by looking. (I can't help but imagine this as mystical laser-beam technology.)

The story continues from there—the two are eventually placated by the sight of an old man piously gathering wood to prepare for Shabbat. But the part that has always stuck with me (and many others) is those laser beams.

> "I will not come to terms . . . never take my eyes off and retreat."—SR

That pure light of prophetic indignation, equally activated by the structures of a colonialist government, and the perceived waning of his own people's spiritual engagement. Judgment, incendiary, with its power to cut through the illusions of this world, but also to destroy this world in the process.

This double-edged incandescence thrums in your words. You are luminous when you speak of what you deem good (reading the Bhagavad Gita beside the letters of St. Paul;

social justice; your family) and cuttingly fierce in your critique of evil (imperialism; Islamophobia.) For what you find merely distasteful (the Dalai Lama; Toni Morrison; novels in general) you dial it down to a withering dismissal.

(Side note: if I'm going to out you for talking shit about Toni Morrison, I will also hasten to say that your awareness of racism in America is a beacon, clear-eyed and uncompromising. "When I speak about American Blacks," you write, "I am talking about a grave, a criminal injustice done to them as a people which must be righted." [14/11/90]).

Your approach to spirituality is vatic, radical; impatient with orthodoxy, but ready to be transported by beauty and insight. Dear Shreela, I don't need to tell you that prophecy is famously difficult for the inhabitants of a town to hear. After all, the point of prophecy is to call into question the actions of said inhabitants.

> "I don't think any power on earth at the moment can stop this insane country . . . I have been trying to say so here and whenever I return to India, but I don't think people believe me either because I'm a woman or an unconventional one, or it is some sort of snobbery that I don't understand." (*letter of 17/11/90*)

In the great tradition of spiritual radicals, you are willing to risk going too far—as in your cheerful "self-conversion" to Islam, as a protest against Islamophobia. Admirable in intention, maybe a little questionable ethically, as, with seemingly little study or preparation, your next move is to speak for that religion in the public forum:

Did I tell you that I am a self-convert to Islam. By that I mean that as long as I live in the US and there are communal wars in India, but most specially because the viciously racist treatment by the US against Arabs and Islam I've decided to exist like a bee in the bonnet; to make them think, to startle them out of their smugness . . .. Last fall I attended a meeting to discuss how to deal with congressional threats to cut off funds for the arts because of some alleged misuse of funds for 'pornography'. I argued the devil's advocate in that taxpayer's money should not be so used and also what about blasphemy I being Muslim, what would happen. There was a gasp followed by a horrendous silence. These were college educated professionals mind you, and supposedly quite worldly. I don't think that anyone had ever seen a Muslim in real life, and I was their first. (*letter of 1/4/91*)

This passage is made even more notable by the fact that a couple paragraphs earlier, you write quite nonchalantly about the "quite superb if I say so myself" paschal lamb you'd cooked for some friends to celebrate Easter.

Still, I wish I could have seen you at the community meeting about arts funding, where you went "To startle them out of their smugness." Classic prophecy.

Your passion for sacred text. Your voracious desire to see patterns which transcend specific traditions and map human spiritual experience. Your sense that the world speaks to and through you—these make you a prophet.

"The essence of things call me sister," you write. A prophet is a prophet. She cannot stop being what she is. When the world calls you sister, you have no choice but to answer. I will close with your own words.

Give me the courage to use your knife
and furrow into the deep earth of my own body
and see with the eye of a grub, a God dancing like a God
to the sound of my mere breath coming to a stop.
—SR, *Address Before an Empty Assembly*

AJR

....

ALICIA JO RABINS is an award-winning writer, composer, performer and Torah teacher. She is the author of two poetry books, *Divinity School* (winner of the *American Poetry Review/ Honickman First Book Prize*) and *Fruit Geode* (finalist for the Jewish Book Award), and is the recipient of grants and fellowships from Bread Loaf, Lower Manhattan Cultural Council, and Oregon Literary Arts. An internationally touring musician, Rabins is the creator and performer of *Girls in Trouble*, an indie-folk song cycle about women in Torah, and the independent mystical-musical feature film, *A Kaddish for Bernie Madoff*. www.aliciajo.com

THIS EDITION OF THE UNSUNG MASTERS
IS PRODUCED AS A COLLABORATION AMONG:

Gulf Coast: A Journal of Literature and Fine Arts
and
Copper Nickel
Pleiades: Literature in Context
The Asian American Literary Review
The Georgia Review

GENEROUS SUPPORT AND FUNDING PROVIDED BY:

The Nancy Luton Fund
University of Houston Department of English
University of California, San Diego

This book is set in Marion with Avenir
and Manifesto titles and Poiret One page numbers.